THE
99
CRITICAL SHOTS

THE 99 CRITICAL SHOTS IN POOL

RAY MARTIN
Champion of the World
and
ROSSER REEVES

Drawings by Harry Zelenko
Photographs by Walter Becchio

Times
BOOKS

All rights reserved under International and Pan-American Copyright Conventions. Published in the United States by Times Books, a division of Random House, Inc., New York, and simultaneously in Canada by Random House of Canada Limited, Toronto.

Library of Congress Cataloging in Publication Data

Martin, Ray, 1935-
    The 99 critical shots in pool.
  1.   Pool (Game)   I. Reeves, Rosser, joint author.
II. Title.
GV893.M37   794.7'3   75-36260
ISBN 0-8129-0618-7 (hardcover)
ISBN 0-8129-6313-X (paper)

Manufactured in the United States of America

Designed by Nicholas Krenitsky

10 9 8 7

Dedicated to

BARBARA MARTIN
RUSSELL MILLER
and
COMMANDER JAMES F. ROOHAN JR.

CONTENTS

PREFACE

There is a famous phrase in pool called "Shooting the Lights Out!" In straight pool, this means that a player is running rack after rack. He sinks fourteen balls without a miss, leaves the fifteenth ball on the table as his "break ball," reracks the balls, breaks the rack, and starts running the balls again.

The world's high run record is 625 balls!*

Not one player in a hundred can sink five, six, or seven balls without a miss—and yet, *it is easily within his power.* He simply hasn't learned to "cut" balls, "throw" balls, use right and left English, draw balls, bank balls, set up key balls and break balls, get frozen balls off a cushion, use kiss shots, reverse draw, jump shots, "ghost ball" shots, or shoot curved shots. He doesn't understand the Double Kiss, Semi-Massé Shots, Off-the-Cushion Shots, Cushion-First Shots, Cheat-the-Pocket Shots, or how speed affects English, or affects the very angle of his shots.

Yet a high percentage of these shots are very simple to learn. *Some of them (See Shot No. 12, Shot No. 48, Shot No. 50, Shot No. 52, and Shot No. 57 of this book) are so simple that they take hardly any practice at all to learn!* You simply have to be able to recognize them, and then even if you are a bad player you can almost automatically sink the ball!

* In the opinion of the authors, who have examined the evidence, this record is held by Michael Eufemia, who made this run on a 4¼ x 9 table at the Logan Billiard Academy in Brooklyn, on February 2, 1960. The occasion was a pre-scheduled match attended by a standing-room only audience. Over 50 of the witnesses gave their names and addresses, attesting to the above.

Willie Mosconi ran 526 balls on a 4 x 8 table, in 1954, at the East High Billiards Club in Springfield, Ohio.

Why aren't all of these shots in one, or all, of the many books on pool? Why aren't many of them known to men who have made a hobby of pool for years? I think the answer may be that the professionals, who play in competition for money, view them as secrets. They won't even tell each other, if they discover a remarkable new play.

You may doubt this, but the fact remains that *a high percentage of these shots are not in any other books at all.*

A mathematician once estimated that there are 54 *quadrillion* possible shots in pool. Perhaps. But Ray Martin, Champion of the World, after 25 years of play began to observe that nearly all of these fall into well-defined patterns, and that most of them, with minor variations, repeat themselves again and again. Some, as we have said, are so automatic that you can teach them to a five-year-old child in five minutes. Even the most difficult can be mastered by an average player.

These shots, including some of Ray Martin's own special secrets, are what he has put in this book.

Equally as important as these "critical shots" is another thing known to only a few players and that is—*positional play.* You sink, let us say, ball "A". Can you control the cue ball so that it goes to just the right spot in front of ball "B", so that you have an easy shot?

Ray Martin once jokingly said:

Pool is very simple. Just sink one ball after another, and *make sure each time* that your cue ball stops where you have an easy shot!

That is positional play, and it is a key *motif* in this book. "I've got my cue ball on a string today," you will hear a player say, which means: "I am controlling the cue ball so that one shot leads easily to another." If anything, cue ball control is the key to the finest pool.

No one book can tell you all about positional play—but once you have learned these "99 Critical Shots," you will have a very good idea of where that cue ball is going to go.

Rosser Reeves

THE
99
CRITICAL SHOTS

SOME OTHER ARTS BEHIND THE SHOTS

THE TABLE

The pool table today is a triumph of design and engineering skill. The lustrous cloth is stretched over an absolutely flat bed of polished slate, which in turn is perfectly balanced in relation to the floor.

The cloth. is wool, or a mixture of wool and nylon. Brush this cloth carefully before a game, to make sure there are no bits of fluff, or dirt; and when you brush, brush from the head of the table to the foot, to make sure that you keep the nap smooth.

Ray Martin shooting

The playing area of the table is known as *the bed,* i.e., the cloth, the rails along the inner edge, and the pockets. The head of the table is where you find the manufacturer's name plate. The opposite end, where the balls are racked, is the foot. Set in the rail are 18 dots, or diamonds, to help you calculate your shots.

All tables are twice as long as they are wide, and come in three sizes: 4 x 8 feet, 4½ x 9 feet, and 5 x 10 feet. The standard table today is the 4½ x 9, with a playing area of 100 x 50 inches. The corner pockets are from 4⅞ to 5⅛ inches wide. The side pockets, which are wider, are from 5⅜ inches to 5⅝ inches.

THE BALLS

All play today is with the new, modern composition balls. Solid, heavy, and perfectly rounded, they have displaced the old ivory balls of the last century. They weigh from 5½ to 6 ounces, and measure 2¼ inches in diameter.

Balls 1 through 8 are a single color, numbered, but without a band. Balls 9 through 15 are white with a broad colored band equidistant from the numbers on each side. The cue ball is white.

It makes a difference, in shooting, to have clean balls. Wash with soap and water before an important game, perhaps applying a little plastic polish, just as you brush down the cloth to make it spotless and smooth.

The whole table sparkles and shines when you give it proper care.

Close-up of a rack of highly polished balls—taken to reflect the shine and the highlights

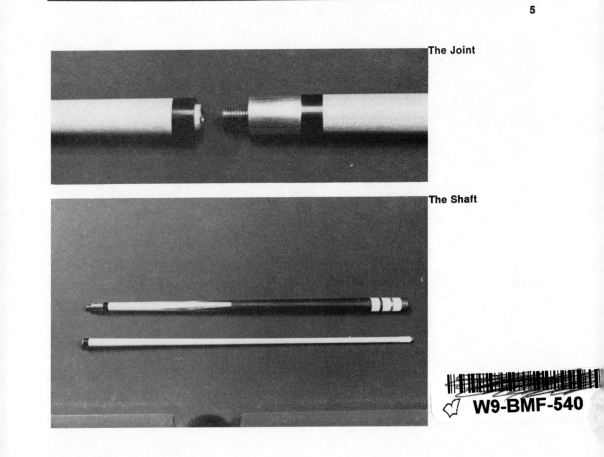

The Joint

The Shaft

THE CUE

The cue, to a pool player, is what a Stradivarius is to a violinist, or a rifle to a great wing shot. It adds music to marksmanship. It is an extension of the player's arm, his brain, his reflexes, and his skill. It must feel *right* in his hand. It must be perfectly balanced. It must not be too light or too heavy. It must be so smooth that, on the stroke, it slides through his fingers like silk.

The player takes jealous care of his cue. He unscrews it, after each game, and puts it carefully in its case. He polishes the shaft (so precious is it), or rubs it smooth with 600-A sandpaper, which is so fine that it feels like a baby's skin. He guards it against nicks.

And, if he is a fine player, he won't let anybody else shoot with it.

It is a fine tool.

To put another in his hand (heavier, lighter, or differently balanced) means that he must adjust all of his delicate reflexes.

The standard length of the cue is 57 inches. The width of the ferrule is 10 to 13 millimeters; but most professionals use 13 millimeters, because it gives them a bigger hitting surface on the tip. Depending on the *feel* of it to the individual player, most professionals use a cue that weighs between 19½ and 21 ounces.

You can get a cue which is just right for you, for a low price. Or, you may go to a custom cue maker and pay hundreds of dollars for a magnificent work of art, made with rare woods and superb inlays.

Take your choice—but cherish it!*

* One cue maker, Herman J. Rambow, was elected to the Billiard Hall of Fame. It was Herman who perfected the jointed cue by inserting a countersunk screw in the recessed butt end, making a strong and perfect connection.

In the opinion of the authors, the greatest cue maker since Herman Rambow is George Balabushka. He became a legend during his lifetime and died December 4, 1975 in Brooklyn. A Balabushka cue, like a Stradavarius violin, is today among the most valued in existence. Among the top players who use Balabushka cues are: Steve Mizerak, Jean Balukas, Joe Balsis, Jim Rempe, Cisero Murphy, Pete Margo, Willie Mosconi and Ray Martin.

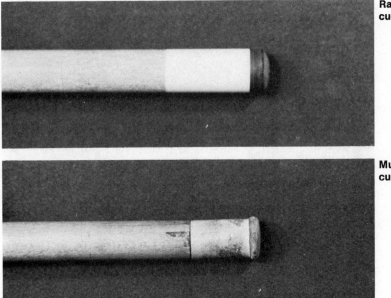

Ray Martin's cue tip

Mushroomed cue tip

THE TIP

It pays to remember that *all the magic you put on the cue flows through the leather tip!* If you let your tip deteriorate, your game will deteriorate. Accuracy disappears. You begin to miscue. You can't control the spin on the ball.

Most professionals prefer a hard leather tip, but one with a surface soft enough to permit a slight roughening, so that the chalk will hold to the leather. Is it too hard and glossy? Then brush it lightly with sandpaper, to roughen it up. Or, roll it very lightly on a rough file. But never, ever scrape it!

In the top picture on the left we show the tip on Ray Martin's cue. Notice that it is high, and slightly rounded on the end. Notice that the leather is even with the sides of the ferrule. Professionals sandpaper the sides, to prevent the tip from spreading. They wet the sides with their fingers, to harden it, and then polish the sides with leather, or the back of sandpaper.

Now look at the cue tip below, a public cue taken from a New York club. It has spread, and mushroomed out over the shaft. The top is hard, and slick. It is a disaster!

**Close-up
of hand using
the chalk cube**

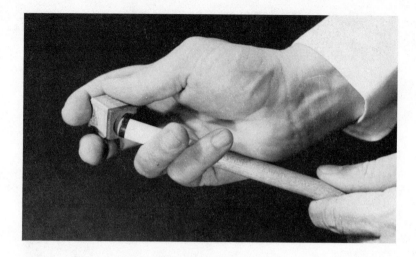

THE CHALK

Watch Ray Martin shoot, and you'll discover that *he chalks his
cue after almost every shot.* For if there's no chalk on the leather,
the leather just can't grip the ball.

Use a fresh chalk cube. If the tip has hollowed out a deep
cavern, the chalk won't spread evenly. Chalk, and then look at
the tip. Is there still a shiny spot? A shiny edge? Fill it in. And
don't grind the chalk cube heavily down on the tip. You will
flatten out the tip's soft roughness, and make it slippery and hard.

Above all, don't forget to chalk!

THE BASIC BRIDGE

It is impossible to shoot a good game of pool without what is
known as a good "hand bridge." Notice the photographs above,
showing the hands of Ray Martin.

The cue slides securely through a channel made by the thumb
and forefinger. The widespread fingers, fanned out on the table
below, provide a solid and immovable base. Yet the cue moves
through this channel easily and smoothly, with no pulling against
the flesh, and no tendency to waver and get out of line.

Since the precise placement of the cue tip on the ball is of
major importance, take time out to master this basic bridge.
Since you will use it in about 80 percent of your shots, do it
until it comes naturally. Form it until your fingers channel the
cue easily and naturally, without muscular strain. It is a precision bridge—one of the keys to precision shooting.

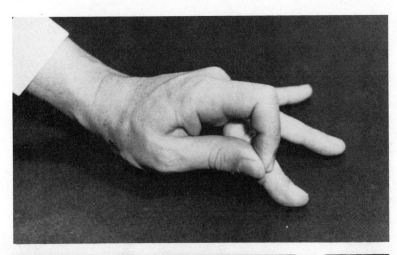

The basic bridge
showing the front
of the hand

The basic bridge
showing the back
of the hand

Many books give columns of tedious text on the exact placement of the fingers. We believe a photograph is enough.

You will find that you can raise the channel high for a Follow
Shot, and drop the channel low for a Draw Shot. Some players
with big hands, for a Draw Shot, bend the middle finger under,
as shown in the right photograph below.

When shooting over another ball, use the "V" bridge to get the
proper elevation. Spread the fingers widely to make a firm base.
You will find that if you bring up the thumb, you get more
security for the cue stroke.

When the cue ball is close to the rail, shoot between the first two
fingers after folding back your thumb. Notice that the forefinger
and the thumb are making a channel to keep your stroke accurate.

**Hand with cue
in channel**

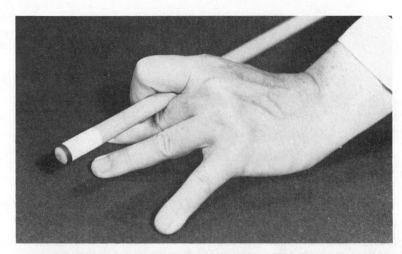

**Hand high for a
Follow Shot**

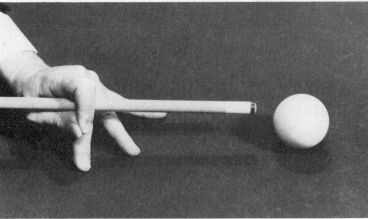

**Hand low for a
Draw Shot**

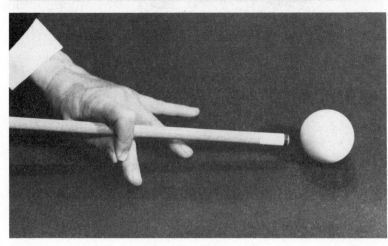

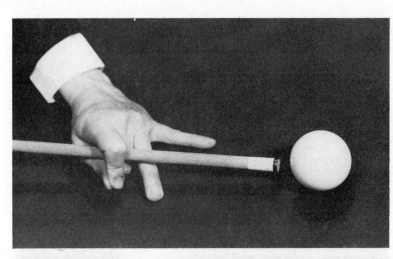

For some people, a bent finger for a Draw Shot

The high "V" bridge

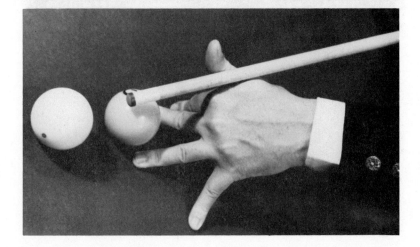

The rail bridge with thumb tucked under

Close-up of the butt, showing how the cue is held for the mechanical bridge

(opposite)
Shot of Ray Martin using the mechanical bridge, showing grip, bridge on rail, and the arm up

THE MECHANICAL BRIDGE

For making long shots, it is necessary to use the mechanical bridge. Since the action here comes mostly from the wrist, grip the cue stick between the thumb and the index finger. If you wrap your whole hand around the butt, it will spoil the delicacy of your aim.

Lay the mechanical bridge flat on the table, to keep it firm and steady. Notice that Ray Martin is sighting right down the cue, like a rifle barrel, with his elbow well up. Notice also that one hand is on the bridge to hold it firmly.

THE GRIP

It is a sad fact, but 9 out of 10 beginning players grip the cue in either of two wrong ways. They choke it in too firm a grip, with all five fingers wound tightly around the butt—killing their delicate wrist action and spoiling all fluidity in their shots. Or they grip the cue too delicately between their thumb and forefinger, which spoils power and control.

The key to a smooth, fluent stroke is to *grip the cue firmly, yet lightly, with your thumb, index and middle fingers.* The keynote is "firmly, yet lightly." You then have all the power you need for hard shots, and all the softness and delicacy you need for soft shots. You have eliminated unnecessary muscular strain.

No matter what shot you make—soft, hard, or medium—grip the cue the same way!

Beginners, too, are prone to another deadly error. They grip the cue too far forward or too far back. Keep in mind that the cue should be balanced in the hand, so that it has a right "feel". First find the fulcrum of your cue, the exact point of balance. Simply balance it on one finger. Then slide your hand back from 4 to 7 inches behind this balance point, until the cue feels right and easy in your hand.

When you do it right, you will find that the cue becomes an unconscious extension of your eye, arm and brain.

**Wrong—
the rigid clench**

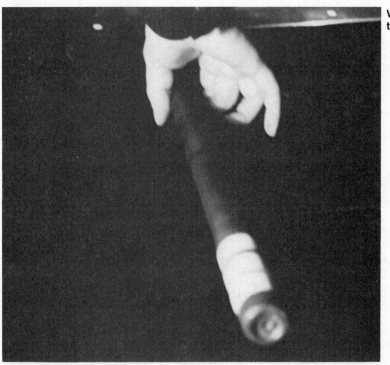

Wrong—
the "butterfly!"

Right—
the thumb and
three fingers

Ray Martin stand-
ing with the cue
stick almost
touching the ball
on the spot, feet
properly apart

THE STANCE

It is impossible to over-emphasize the importance of a *correct
stance*. When you have it, you are comfortable, well-balanced,
firm on your feet, relaxed—sighting down the cue like sighting
down a rifle barrel, ready for some deadly shots.

Without a correct stance you are unsteady, wavering, teeter-
ing. What's more, you are bringing into play a whole battery of
muscles that you don't need to make the shot. You are draining
yourself and fighting the shot.

Try this:

Put the cue ball on the spot. Lay the cue over the rail, until
the cue almost touches the ball, as shown in the first photograph.
This is the correct distance from the table.

Now, drop your right foot back until the toe is about in the
middle of your left foot, at the same time turning the toe of your
right foot slightly to the right (roughly 30°). Now bend forward
at the hips, which means bending your left leg—but *keep your
right leg straight*. As you bend and shift the center of gravity
forward, you will find that to be comfortable you will also be
turning your left foot slightly to the right. You are now bending

forward with your weight evenly distributed on both feet, and you can lean forward into the stroke.

As you lean forward, however, keep your weight on both feet. If you shift it too much to the front leg, which is bent, then big muscles must support you. If you shift it too much to the back leg, you will feel a strain coming straight up into the pelvis. On both feet, however, you are in an easy and solid position.

Now, with your left arm straight, or almost so, make your hand bridge on the table. You will find that you are solid, easy and relaxed—resting on a natural tripod. What is more, your right arm is swinging close to your side, ready for the automatic "pendulum" which we are going to discuss in a moment, and which is important in a great stroke.

Bend forward until your head is fairly low over the cue, sighting down the cue like a rifle barrel, directly in line with the shot.

You're ready!

Obviously, if you have to stretch to make a shot, or make a shot where the cue ball is almost against the cushion in front of you, the elements of your stance will change. Just remember that *balance is the secret,* so that all of your body muscles are relaxed enough to concentrate on the pendulum. Otherwise you will be fighting against your own skill.

Ray in full, correct stance, sighting down over the cue

**SIX ERRORS
THAT RUIN A
PLAYER'S STANCE**

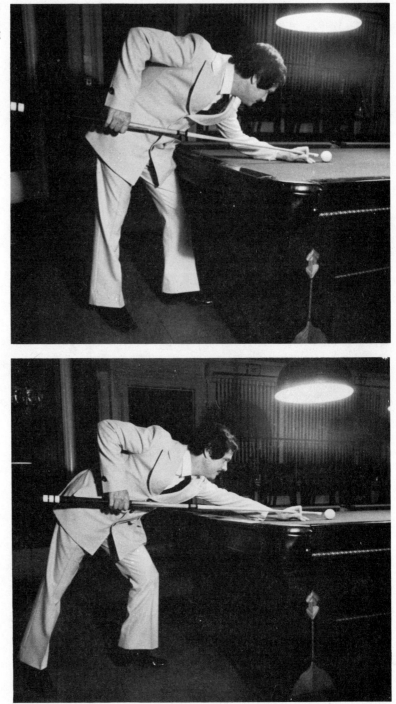

Too close

Too far

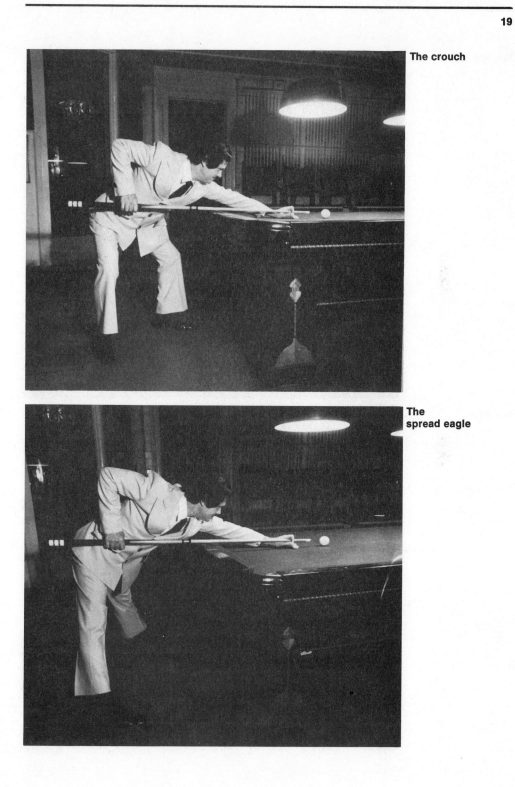

The crouch

The
spread eagle

Too low

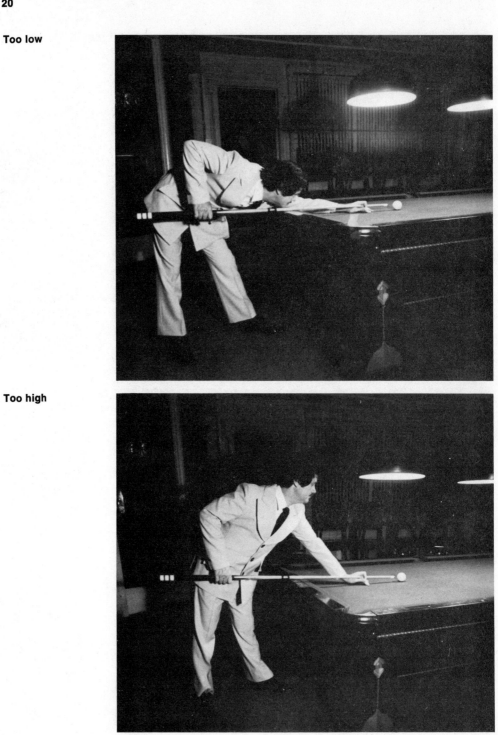

Too high

The Pendulum:
A stop-motion,
retouched picture
showing the swing
of the arm from
the elbow
(see over)

THE STROKE

If there is a key to great pool, an *essence* to great pool, it is—
the stroke! In golf, a 12-year-old-girl, with a good swing, can
drive a ball further and more accurately than a 200-pound athlete
with a bad swing. It is not muscle, but form; it is not clumsiness,
but grace; it is not hit-and-miss, but precision. And so it is in
great pool.

Assume you are in position. Your stance and your bridge are
proper. Your cue is chalked, and you have the proper grip. Your
eyes are directly over the line of the cue and ball. You are
balanced and relaxed. At this point two elements come into play:

(1) Your pendulum, the swing of your arm from your elbow.

(2) Your follow-through, your "stroking" of the ball.

Actually one is part of the other, but it will help if we discuss
them almost as though they were separate things.

The Pendulum: Your forearm is swinging closely to your side,
like a pendulum swung from your shoulder. The cue motion, as
you can see from the photograph, is partly in the wrist and
partly in the arm. However, your motions are fluid. Neither your
hand nor your wrist is cramped. The pendulum is swinging back

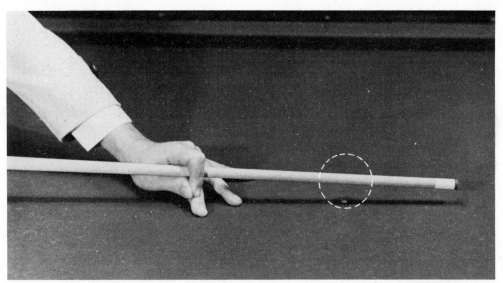

The Follow-Through: A retouched picture showing the cue full back in the hand bridge, with a ghost cue going through and beyond the ball

and forward—*a fixed rhythm* ready to deliver the cue tip to the proper part of the ball, *so fixed and so automatic that you can actually shut your eyes and make the shot!*

This is not rhetoric. Ray Martin, to prove this, having once gotten set, can turn his head and make a perfect shot *without seeing the ball.**

The Stroke: But a perfect pendulum is only the beginning. Just as, in golf, a player swings through the ball, so in pool *a player strokes through the ball.* He shoots with a smooth, flowing follow-through, as though the ball were not even there; and *the cue increases in speed until contact, and then comes to a natural stop.*

Let us repeat: the cue comes to a natural stop. It is not stopped by any "pulling" of the cue, but simply because the cue tip has reached the end of the stroke. Pulling causes flinching, inadvertent cue tip movement and loss of accuracy.

Hence the words: "He has a good stroke." "He's in dead stroke." "He's free-stroking."

It is important to remember, in developing a full stroke, that too long a backswing may make the cue tip swerve. Too short a backswing, and the stroke won't have an effortless follow-through —and come easily to a natural stop.

* A perfect pendulum also enables a player to keep his eye on the object ball. This is the way he shoots. *He never keeps his eye on the cue ball on the last stroke.*

THE 99 CRITICAL SHOTS

In every person who engages in a manual art or skill there is an "eye, arm and brain computer". As one practices, the data is fed into a memory bank; and suddenly, the artless becomes artful; the impossible becomes possible; and suddenly the most incredible shots are accomplished with unconscious ease.

So it is with pool. And if you know the *theory* before you practice, your skill grows with many times the speed.

These shots were selected as critical because underlying them is the entire *theory* of the game.

What is more, theory aside, you must make nearly all of these specific shots, in one way or another, within the next one hundred games—or you will not be playing a good game.

Ray Martin

KEY TO THE DIAGRAMS

The cue ball is the ball you strike with the cue. Each cue ball is a white circle, like this:

The ball you wish to sink into the pocket (which may or may not be the *object ball,* i.e., the ball hit by the cue ball) is black, like this:

If there are other balls on the table, they are gray, like this:

If we show a spot to which a ball *may* go, it is a dotted circle, like this:

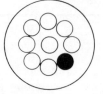

In most diagrams, the cue stick is shown, to make clear the direction of the shot, like this:

In most of the shots, we show a "clock face," which shows the point at which the cue stick should hit the cue ball, like this:

If the balls were shown in actual size, in relation to the size of the table, they would be too small. We are using, for case of understanding *an enormously enlarged ball.* However, if you will measure from the diamonds on the rail you will get an exact enough measurement, like this:

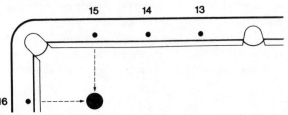

Warning! In reading the text, when you read "hit the object ball to the left," or "to the right," *imagine you are standing on the same side of the table as the cue.*

We use three speeds in this book: soft, medium, and hard. Unless we specify otherwise, shoot with medium speed.

One More Thing: "The 99 Critical Shots in Pool" should be read in sequence, unless you are already an experienced player. One shot unfolds naturally into another shot, and assumes that you know principles and terminology used earlier.

These shots are really an interlocking series of lessons, and short of the presence of the master (to explain mistakes and correct you on matters of form) they are the closest thing to studying under Ray Martin.

Every single one of these shots, in one form or another, you will use over and over again in winning pool.

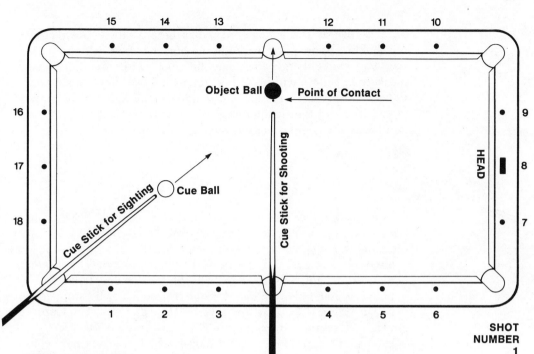

THE CUT SHOT

The best way to start a book on pool is to discuss the most frequent shot in pool, and that happens to be—the Cut Shot. To sink the black object ball above, the cue ball must "cut" it, i.e., hit it at an angle.

The question is, *at what point should the two balls make contact?*

Sight down your cue stick, through the direct center of the black object ball and *into the pocket.* Directly in front of your cue tip, you will "see" an imaginary spot. That is the point of contact (see that little black dot?). *If the two balls meet on this dot, the black object ball will roll into the center of the pocket.*

Right away, however, we have a problem: *If you aim the cue ball directly at this point, you will never hit it!*

Study the diagram below:

Here we have aimed right through the cue ball at the point of contact, but as you can see from the dotted circle, we didn't hit it. Because of the curvature of the balls, we hit well to the left of it. We would have missed the pocket!

So obviously, the "point of contact" is *not* the "point of aim."

How do you determine the "point of aim"?

There are as many home remedies here as there are recipes for cooking. Some players divide the object ball into 1, ½, ¼, ⅛, ⅟₁₆, ⅟₃₂, etc. Others (who may be good with divining rods) measure in cue-tip widths. Others see imaginary "luminous spots." Others (see below) picture an imaginary cue ball touching the object ball and the two pointing into the pocket (about as good an idea as any), and shoot the cue ball to fill this space:

Point of Aim

There is only one true solution: Start sinking balls! Set up ball after ball, in front of pocket after pocket, and—sink balls! Set up the same shot again and again and—sink balls!

Suddenly the eye and the brain begin to take over, and you begin to *sink balls*. So start! Sink balls! Sink balls! Sink balls!

It's very much like the old story of the woman who stopped a man carrying a violin case and asked: "How do you get to Carnegie Hall?" And the musician said: "Practice! Practice! Practice!"

We hate to start a book with a shot in which we can't help you. However, we have better news later on.

Note: See Shot No. 26 for "The Cut Shot with English."

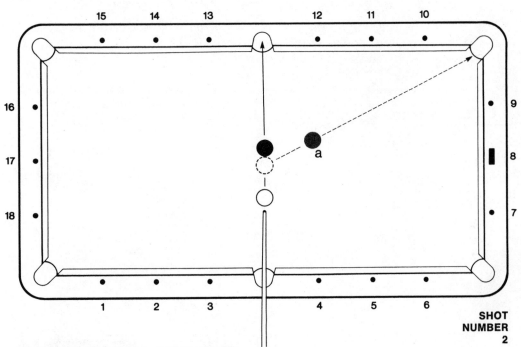

THE CENTER BALL STOP SHOT

Place the cue ball and the object ball six inches apart in front of the side pocket. Strike the cue ball with medium speéd. Since the cue ball slides the full six inches, it does not pick up from the cloth any forward roll at all. Thus, *the full energy of the cue ball is transferred to the object ball, and the cue ball stops dead where it hits*, in direct line for ball "A". (Already, you are playing position!)

This shot—which is of crucial importance—calls for a *dead center hit on the cue ball* and *a dead center hit on the object ball*. Otherwise, your cue ball will skitter off to the right or left, spoiling your direct shot on ball "A". Even worse, you may miss the pocket!

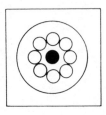

Most cue balls have a little dot on the ball. Put the cue ball on the table so that this dot is facing you, exactly in the center:

Now chalk your cue, and strike the ball in the center. If the

Note: The beginning player is apt to believe that striking the cue ball in the center is easy. Not so! Thousands of players miss millions of shots, unaware that it is not their aim which is at fault, but the fact that they are hitting the cue ball off center.

chalk is on the dot, splendid! You will be amazed how many times you hit to the right, left, top, or bottom.

And when you practice the "dot test," practice it this way:

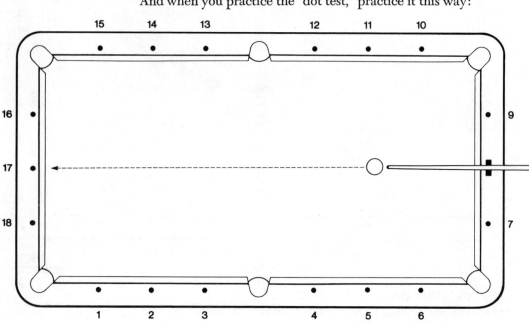

Put the cue ball on the head spot, and shoot it down to the center diamond. See if you can hit the diamond, and have the cue ball return to the tip of your cue!

The beginning player can do this rarely. Ray Martin can do it 20 out of 20 times.

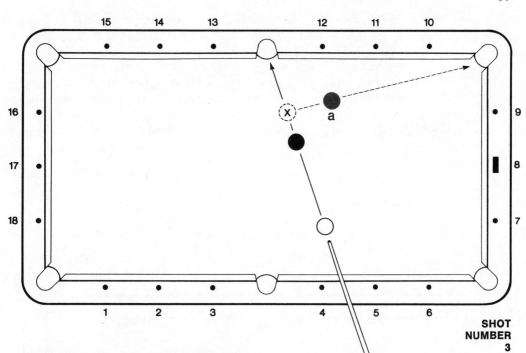

SHOT
NUMBER
3

THE CENTER BALL FOLLOW SHOT

In Shot No. 2 we said: "Since the cue ball slides the full six inches, it does not pick up any forward roll at all."

"Slide" vs. "roll" is an important phenomenon in all center ball shots.

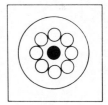

When you first strike the cue ball in dead center, it simply *slides* forward over the fabric: it has no forward spin, because it is not turning at all. But when you shoot a short shot slowly, or a long shot with more speed, something happens. The friction of the fabric on the ball takes over, and the ball begins to *roll forward,* turning a Center Ball Stop Shot into a Follow Shot.

Here is what happens:

The cue ball picks up forward momentum of its own, and continues to roll forward after it hits the object ball.

In this Center Ball Follow Shot, the balls are not six inches apart, as in Shot No. 2, *but two feet apart.* You want the cue ball to roll a few inches beyond the object ball, to give you a perfect position on ball "A." Hit with a medium stroke,* dead center.

---

* In this book we use three speeds of strokes—soft, medium, and hard. Tables differ, fabrics differ, so each reader must experiment. Practice the above shot until the cue ball rolls just the right distance. You will then be shooting with medium speed.

Since it is a short distance, by the time the cue ball reaches the object ball, it will have picked up just enough forward roll to go on to "X".

Obviously, if you shot a perfect center ball a longer distance, and at the same speed, there would be more and more forward roll.

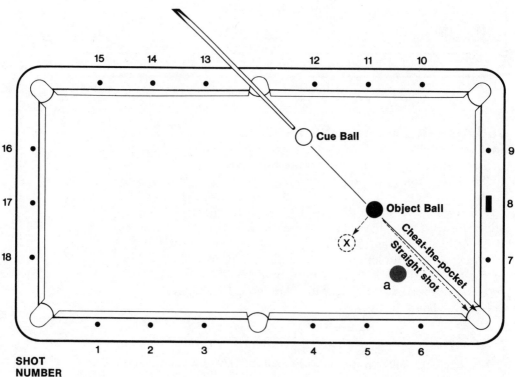

SHOT
NUMBER
4

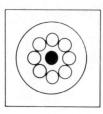

CENTER BALL CHEAT-THE-POCKET SHOT

As you can see from the diagram, the cue ball and the object ball are lined up straight on the corner pocket. When they are lined up like this, and you shoot the cue ball straight ahead, you have Shot No. 2.

In the case above, you want to go off on an angle, to position "X", where you will have an easy shot on ball "A".

The solution is simple: *Cheat the pocket*. Since the pocket is wider than one ball, don't shoot the object ball straight in. Instead, hit the object ball a fraction to the right, so that the object ball will go *slightly* to the left. *This creates an Angle Shot, and your cue ball goes over to "X", making your shot on ball "A" an easy one.*

Notice, you are already beginning to "play position" in pool!

However, since the angle here is a very small one, stroke the cue ball *hard*.

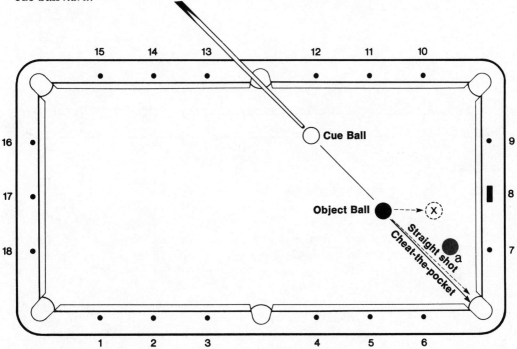

This is exactly the same shot in reverse. By Cheat-the-Pocket Shot from the other side, we deflect the cue ball in the opposite direction.

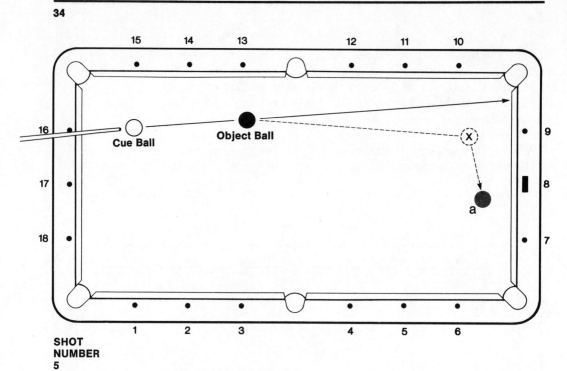

15   14   13   12   11   10

16

Cue Ball   Object Ball   X

9

17   a   8

18   7

1   2   3   4   5   6

**SHOT
NUMBER
5**

THE FOLLOW SHOT

We have seen earlier how a Center Ball Shot slowly turns into a Follow Shot because of the friction of the cloth on the ball.

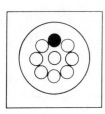

Here we do not rely on friction, but *put follow on the ball with the cue,* by hitting the cue ball at 12:00 o'clock. From the moment the cue touches it, the ball has forward roll. It is an important positional shot in pool.

Take the above shot as an illustration. Here, as the diagram shows, the cue ball and the object are not "dead on" the pocket. Thus, you must hit the object ball at a slight angle, to sink it.

As you do, apply follow, i.e., shoot at 12:00 o'clock. The cue ball will follow to "X", which puts it in a perfect position to sink ball "A".

Shoot with a medium stroke.

In making this shot, begin to perfect your stroke. *Follow through!* Just as a golf player swings his club *through* the golf ball, let your cue pass right *through* the top of your cue ball, going at least three or four inches beyond. Unless you do this, you are apt to pull or jerk your stroke, which leads to terrible inaccuracies. The good player has a smooth, flowing stroke with follow—through.

This picture illustrates what we mean by "follow through":

Let the cue go completely "through" your ball.

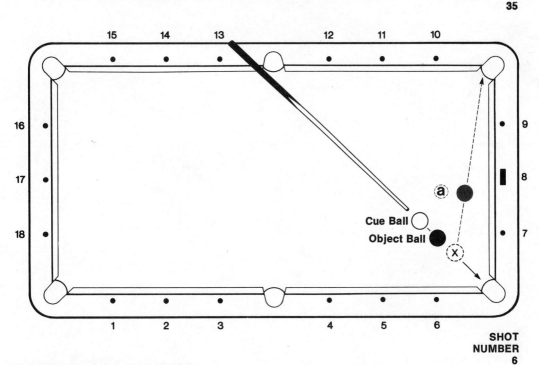

SHOT
NUMBER
6

THE FOLLOW NIP SHOT

When the balls are close together (about one-half ball, or less),
it is impossible to follow through on your stroke. If you do, the
cue ball will rebound from the close object ball, back onto your
cue tip, and the cue tip will hit the cue ball twice, which is a foul.
What is more, your cue ball will then follow the object ball into
the pocket, which is another foul (or "scratch").

If you don't believe it, try the above shot with a follow
through!

The only way to play this is with a Nip Shot. You must jerk the
cue back, after the cue has penetrated the cue ball for about
¼ inch. Shoot at 12:00 o'clock, *with a soft stroke*. The object ball
will roll into the pocket, and the cue ball will stop at "X", giving
you perfect position for sinking ball "A". Notice again that you
are beginning to *play position*, i.e., position your cue ball for the
next shot.

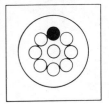

Position play is the secret of fine pool. Later on we will go into
it much more thoroughly. Remember what Ray Martin said in
the preface: "Pool is really very simple. Just sink one ball after
another, making sure *each* time that your cue ball stops where
you have an easy shot!"

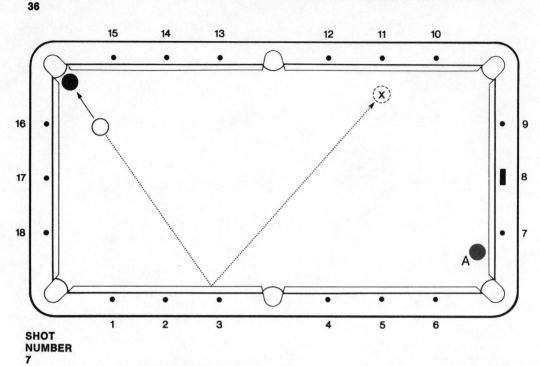

SHOT
NUMBER
7

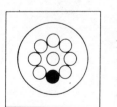

THE DRAW SHOT

The Draw Shot is one of the most elegant and beautiful in pool. A player leans over the table; you hear the sharp "Crack!" of the cue ball against the object ball. Suddenly, the cue ball spins directly backwards—seemingly in defiance of the laws of physics!

What's more, the Draw Shot is one of the great critical shots in pool. *About 50% of your shots will involve draw in one way or another.* It is a shot you must master completely. You must be able to draw automatically, effortlessly.

Set up the balls as shown. Sink the object ball, shooting hard at 6:00 o'clock, and draw the ball back along the dotted line. If you can reach the cushion, good! If you can draw your cue ball to "X" (in position to sink ball "A")—excellent! Your draw is beginning to reach championship calibre, if you can do it every time. (Ray Martin can draw the ball twice the length of the table, making two and even three cushion shots, although these are rarely necessary.)

Do not infer from the above diagram, which is merely an exercise, that draw is used only on straight shots. Consider the shot below, which may come up a dozen times in one game of pool.

You want to sink the object ball, and *come straight down the table after making this angular cut shot.* Apply draw as you sink the object ball, and the cue ball will spin smoothly back to "X"!

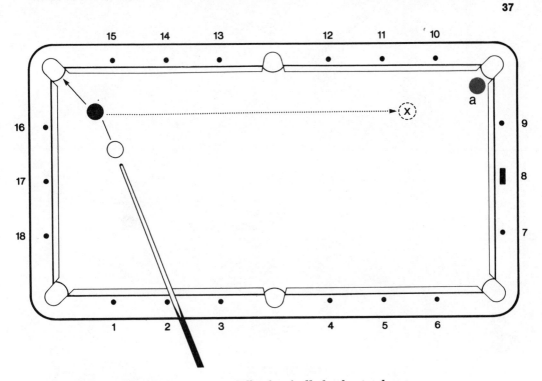

Most players find this the most difficult of all the basic shots, but it will be easy if you remember two things, and learn one little mental trick:

REMEMBER! Follow-through in this shot is most essential. Your cue should pass through the cue ball at least four or five inches, to put extreme back spin on the ball.

REMEMBER! Keep your cue as level as possible, and lower your hand bridge so that the cue passes through the ball at 6:00 o'clock.

THE TRICK! Pretend that there is a "ghost ball" four or five inches in front of your cue ball. Shoot to hit this imaginary ball, as though the cue ball did not exist.

This guarantees full follow-through, and terrific back-spin.

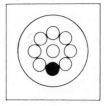

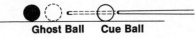

Ghost Ball   **Cue Ball**

The Trick: Shoot "through" your cue ball at an imaginary ball about four or five inches in front of your cue ball. Pretend the cue ball isn't even there! The cue *passes "through" the cue ball,* imparting terrific back spin. And remember, do not elevate the butt of your cue. Keep that cue level!

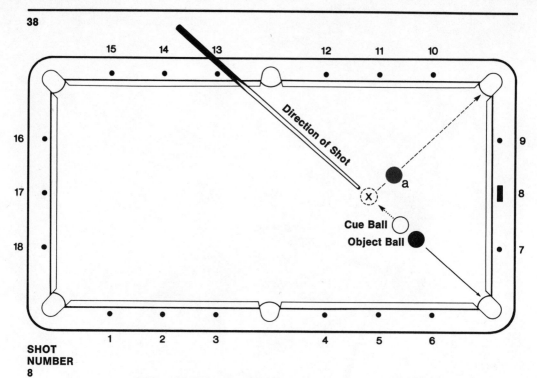

THE DRAW NIP SHOT

Here again (as in Shot No. 6, the Follow Nip Shot) the balls are so close together that you will foul on any attempt to follow through, because your cue tip will hit the cue ball twice, as the cue ball rebounds from the close object ball.

Again, as in Shot No. 6, play a Nip Shot. Jerk the cue back after it has penetrated the cue ball for about ¼ inch. You will find that it is good for about four or five inches of draw, even though the follow-through is non-existent. Your cue ball will draw back to "X". You're playing position again! You have an easy shot on ball "A"!

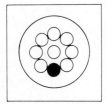

Use a medium speed.

In fact, when you get expert at this Nip Shot, you will find that you can draw back from 18 inches to two feet.

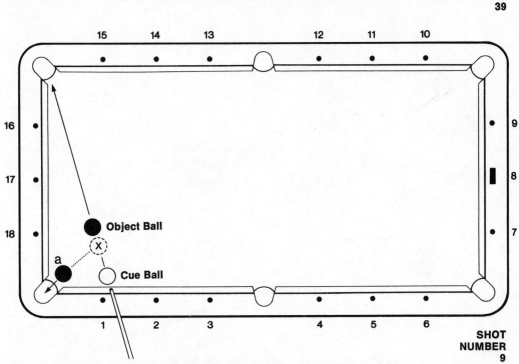

SHOT
NUMBER
9

THE FROZEN-TO-CUSHION DRAW SHOT

In this shot the cue ball is frozen against the cushion. Since only the top part of the ball is peeping over the cushion, you must make a top shot, which means a Follow Shot. And a Follow Shot will carry your cue ball right into the pocket with the object ball. What is the solution?

It's quite simple. Elevate the butt of your cue and *shoot down on the cue ball,* hitting it just as close to the cushion as you can.

Since this is a downward shot, and your cue is pointed to the table top, you can rip the cloth *unless you stop the cue one inch after it hits the ball.*

However, shooting down at this angle will put back-spin on the ball, a bit of draw, so that the cue ball should stop at "X".

Shoot with medium speed. Such a shot should work up to a distance of about three feet.

Remember, *you must shoot about one inch into the cue ball, i.e., it must feel as if your cue tip is actually going into the ball that much.* Of course, as your cue tip goes down that inch, the ball is actually moving out with back-spin.

What is more, you are playing position again, for when the cue ball comes to rest at "X", it is in perfect position to sink ball "A".

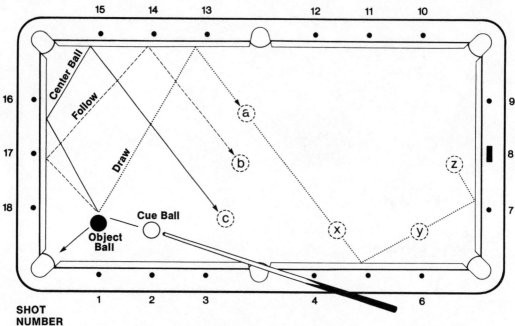

SHOT
NUMBER
10

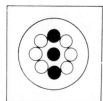

THE 3-WAY POSITION SHOT

Let us repeat again: *Position is the secret of winning pool.* We
have learned only the important variations of the Center Ball
Shot, the Follow Shot, and the Draw Shot—but already we are
beginning to ask ourselves each time: *"Where will the cue ball
stop?"*

Let us now practice a purely positional shot.

Put the object ball and the cue ball parallel to the rail, a distance of three balls from the two diamonds. Shoot the object ball
into the pocket, using center ball, follow, and draw.

Use medium speed.

Look what happens to the cue ball on each shot! You can stop
the cue ball at A, B, or C. More important, depending on what
speed you use, *you can stop the cue ball at any point upon these
three lines, or even beyond.*

Look at the dotted line from A alone. With practice, you can
stop the cue ball at X, Y, or Z.

Study the lines above, and imagine the dozens and dozens of
different positions that you can get, the almost endless number
of positional shots! It all depends on the speed you use, and as
we go through "The 99 Critical Shots in Pool", you will discover
that *speed of stroke* is one of the key factors in position play, and
the behavior of your cue ball.*

---

* We must repeat again, the speeds *soft, medium,* and *hard* are relative.
A new cloth will hold backspin longer. A shiny, worn cloth makes it
very difficult to draw. Thus, on the new cloth you should use a softer
stroke, and on the shiny and worn cloth a harder stroke. Experiment.

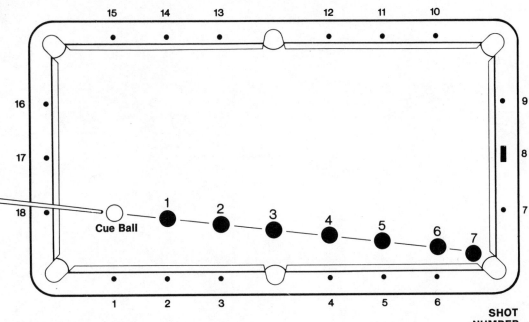

SHOT
NUMBER
11

THE SEVEN BALL STOP SHOT

In Shot No. 2, we showed the Center Ball Stop Shot. It works only at short distances. At longer distances, the friction of the fabric on the ball converts "slide" into "follow."

What, then, is *the perfect stop shot, operating at any distance on the table?* The answer is to shoot at 6:00 o'clock, putting back-spin on the ball, remembering that *the speed you use depends on the distance of the object ball from the pocket.*

The seven object balls shown above, one off each diamond, are the key to this highly critical shot. Start with the cue ball and object ball No. 1. Shoot at 6:00 o'clock, just hard enough to roll the object ball into the pocket, and with just enough back-spin to stop the cue ball dead in its tracks. It takes a little experimenta-tion, but you can find the exact speed within a few minutes.

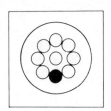

Now go to object ball No. 2, with the cue ball in the same place shown above. You will have to stroke the ball a bit harder.

Now try No. 3 and No. 4. You will find that each time you must shoot harder, and that No. 7 needs a full, hard stroke to carry the back-spin the length of the table, without letting the friction of the cloth diminish the back-spin too much.

Since this shot is one of the most important in pool, you must get to "feel" this gradation in force from soft to hard. Finally, subconsciously, you will *feel* just how hard to stroke the cue ball at 6:00 o'clock to give you a perfect Stop Shot at any distance.

Note: Notice that the draw shot here must also hit exactly on the center line. Otherwise you will be putting angle on the ball, the cue ball will not stop dead in its tracks, and what's more—you'll probably miss the pocket!

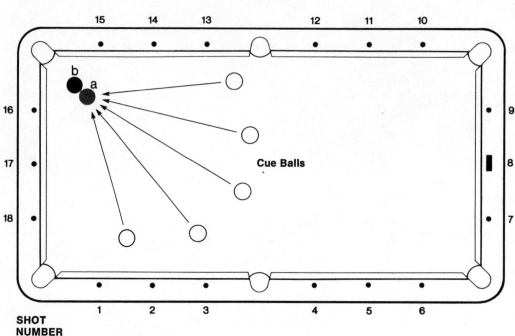

15 14 13 12 11 10

b
a

Cue Balls

16 9
17 8
18 7

1 2 3 4 5 6

SHOT
NUMBER
12

THE DEAD-ON SHOT—CLOSE UP

When two balls touch, they are said to be "frozen." When the two frozen balls point directly into a pocket, they are said to be "dead-on." And when two frozen, dead-on balls are close to the pocket, we observe an interesting phenomenon in pool:

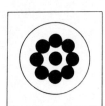

You can hit ball "A" from almost any angle, and shoot from any point on the clock—and ball "B" will roll into the pocket!

Above, we show five cue balls at six different positions. We could show a thousand. Just hit ball "A", and you'll sink ball "B".

The reason is that ball "B" is so close to the yawning pocket it is impossible for anything to go wrong. Experiment, and you will see how extreme your cue ball positions can be.

However, when you move the two frozen, dead-on balls away from the pocket (say, two feet or more) another phenomenon in pool begins to operate, as we shall see in Shot No. 13.

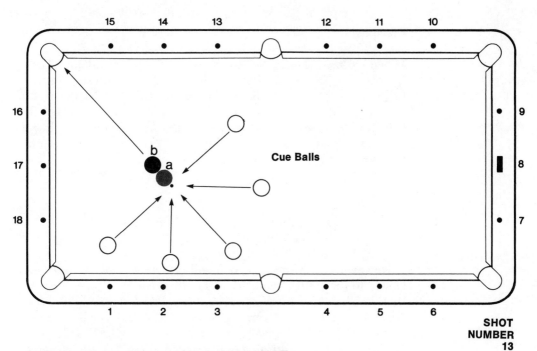

Cue Balls

SHOT
NUMBER
13

THE DEAD-ON SHOT—AT A DISTANCE

Here the two balls are again frozen and dead-on, but they are much further from the pocket. Now no longer, as in Shot No. 12, can you hit ball "A" anywhere. *You must hit ball "A" exactly where you see the little black dot, in the exact center of ball "A".**

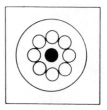

Again the cue ball may come from any direction on one side of ball "A", but if the point of contact is exactly on that dot, the thrust of ball "B" will be directly towards the pocket.

What happens when you miss the dot? We get into another phenomenon of pool known as "throw." Ball "B" will be thrown, and miss the pocket. Unconsciously, we will have to "put English" on ball "B". Before we go into the intricacies of throw, let's discuss English, for without a thorough knowledge of English, you can never be more than mediocre in pool.

---

* When we say "exactly" in the center, keep in mind that the pocket is wider than the ball. Thus, depending on distance, the cue ball may hit ball "A" a hair-line away from center, and still sink ball "B". However, strive for the center! Strive for that little black dot! Don't take a chance!

ENGLISH

When we say "Shoot 7:30" or "Shoot 3:00" we are talking about *putting English on the ball.* Nothing is more confusing to the beginner. Here is why. If you strike the cue ball on the right side, you are using "Right English," yet you are making the ball spin counter-clockwise, or revolve to the *left* as you look down on it. Struck on the left, you are applying "Left English"—yet the ball is revolving to the right:

Right English   Left English
Ball spins to the left   Ball spins to the right

However, if you stand at one end of a table and shoot a ball slowly to the center diamond at the other end, you will discover that *RIGHT ENGLISH MAKES THE BALL VEER TO THE RIGHT* (although it's turning to the left!), and you'll discover that *LEFT ENGLISH MAKES THE BALL VEER TO THE LEFT* (although it's turning to the right!)

Just remember: *The ball veers to the side on which you hit it.* Don't get confused by the direction of the ball's spin.

What's more, English can be communicated from ball to ball. Look at the diagram below, looking straight down on the balls:

If, in the illustration above, you were to hit ball No. 1 in the dead center, it would send ball No. 2 straight ahead. However, when you shoot it *with right English,* here's what happens: (1) The first ball has right English; (2) This imparts to the second ball left English; (3) The second ball, instead of going straight, will slowly veer to the left.

The right English on the cue ball has been converted into left English on the object ball, and the object ball begins to veer left.

This is known as throw.

Throw is English communicated from the cue ball to the object ball, so that the spin on the cue ball is reversed on the object ball, i.e., right English on the cue ball makes the object ball veer left, and vice versa.

In the previous illustration the two balls are not frozen (touch-

ing). The same transfer takes place when the two balls are
frozen:

Nor is it necessary, in some cases, to put English on the cue
ball to impart English to the object ball. If the cue ball is shot
dead center, but hits the second ball on an angle, this angle of
striking will induce spin on the second ball. For example:

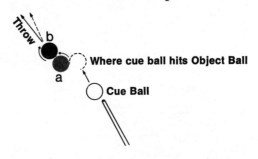

The cue ball is struck, let us say, dead center with no English
imparted from the cue stick. It goes straight ahead, and contacts ball "A" as shown, imparting right English. This right English reverses on ball "B" to become left English, and ball "B" is
thrown to the left.

Now we see why, in Shot No. 13, we must hit the object ball on
that little center dot. Otherwise we would be putting English on
ball "B", and it would be thrown into the cushion rather than
the pocket!

Note: Some people call "follow" and "draw" English. This is incorrect.
Any stroke on the center line of the ball cannot impart the left or right
spin which is English. English = 7:00, 9:00, 10:00, 1:00, 3:00, and
4:00 . . . or anything in between.

Left ⊖ **Right**
English **English**

However, you can put draw or follow on the ball without hitting the exact
center line, in which case you are *combining draw or follow with English.*

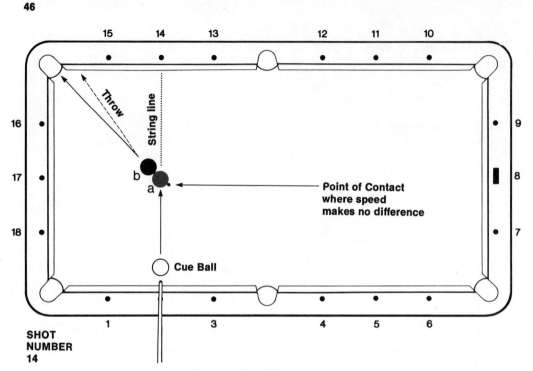

SHOT
NUMBER
14

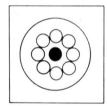

THE HARD THROW SHOT

When you throw a ball, remember one cardinal rule: *The softer you shoot, the more you throw; the harder you shoot, the less you throw.*

Consider the position above. Ball "A" is on the spot. Ball "B" is frozen to it, and both are dead on the center of the pocket (see black arrow). If you shoot the cue ball softly down the string line, it will hit ball "A" straight ahead, putting right English on ball "B" so that it will throw to the right, or down that dotted arrow. *For it is the soft shot that makes English work best, and the essence of throw is English.*

To prove this, shoot the cue ball down the string line *hard.* The English takes to such a minor degree that ball "B" goes into the pocket.*

All this applies in this example only to shooting down the string, which brings the English into play. If ball "A" is hit on the point of contact where you see the little black dot, English will not be involved and ball "B" will automatically roll down the black arrow into the pocket.

---

* Even when you hit the object ball hard, there is still *some* throw. In the first diagram, even with a hard stroke, ball "B" is thrown a distance of about ½ ball. Thanks to the width of the pocket, however, it goes in.

Here is an application of Shot No. 14 from an actual game:

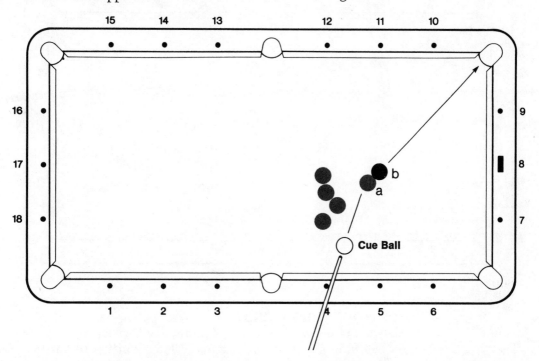

The grey balls hinder the shooter from hitting ball "A" without inducing English and throw. Simply shoot ball "A" *hard,* and ball "B" will make the pocket.

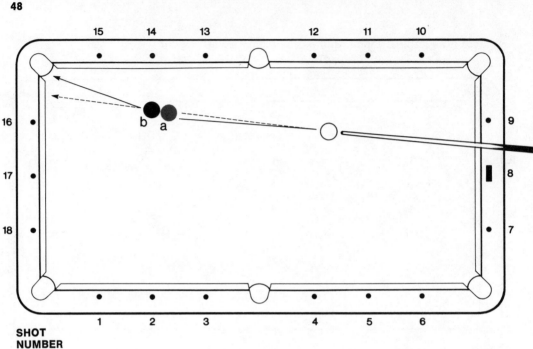

SHOT
NUMBER
15

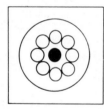

THE SOFT THROW SHOT

Shot No. 14 showed how to avoid throw, and keep a frozen, dead-on ball from going into the cushion. The opposite is to throw a ball (which otherwise would go into the cushion) into the pocket with a soft shot.

Here, as you can see from the dotted line, the two frozen balls are not dead-on the pocket. Ball "B" must be thrown to be sunk, and the solution is simple: Hit ball "A" *softly* on the left side, which puts on left English when the cue ball hits it at that angle. This imparts right English to ball "B", and it is thrown into the pocket.

The solid black line shows the path of the cue ball to the left side of ball "A".

When we are dealing with two frozen balls, there is an added advantage which few players are aware of: *You have a much larger "target area" in hitting the first object ball.*

Consider: When you cut a single ball into a pocket, you must hit the object ball on exactly the right spot, if it is some distance from the pocket. However, with two frozen balls we can hit within an area that is from ¼ to ½ inches wide:

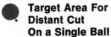

**Target Area For
Distant Cut
On a Single Ball**

**Target Area When
You Throw A
Frozen Ball**

Below is our first diagram of Shot No. 15, except that we have marked out the target area on the object ball. Notice that the cue ball may be in many, many different positions, but as long as they hit the target area, the left English is applied and the throw takes place.

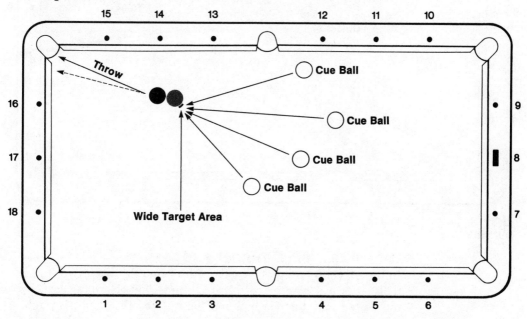

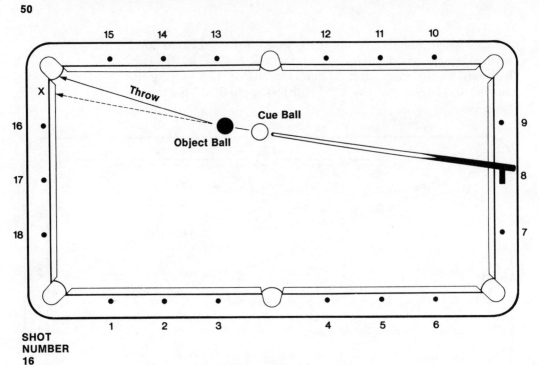

SHOT
NUMBER
16

THE SINGLE BALL THROW SHOT

In the previous two shots, we have discussed throwing two frozen balls. It is just as easy to throw a single ball. Here, as seen by the dotted line, the cue ball and the object ball are not "straight in". (See Glossary, page 219: "Straight in: A shot where the pocket, the object ball, and the cue ball are in a straight line for the pocket.")

Instead, in the case above, the cue ball and the object ball are lined up on the cushion at "X".

If you *cut* (Glossary, page 209) the object ball in, which means hitting it at an angle, the cue ball will go skating off. So, for position's sake, you may wish to throw it in:

1. Aim the cue directly at "X", on the cushion.

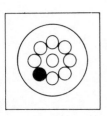

2. Strike the cue ball at 7:30 o'clock, which puts on left English.

3. The cue ball transfers *right* English to the object ball, and the object ball is thrown to the right into the pocket.

When To Throw a Ball. You can *throw* a single ball in, or *cut* a single ball in. How do you decide which to do?

It's position again. We have said that when you *cut* the object ball in, the cue ball goes skating off. When you *throw* it, you *minimize the movement of the cue ball. As you get more expert, you are replacing an angle shot (cut) with a shot which hardly moves the cue ball at all.*

Here is the same position as before. Dotted circle "Y" shows where the cue ball stops with the throw shot. Dotted circle "Z" shows where the cue ball goes skating off *when you don't use throw.*

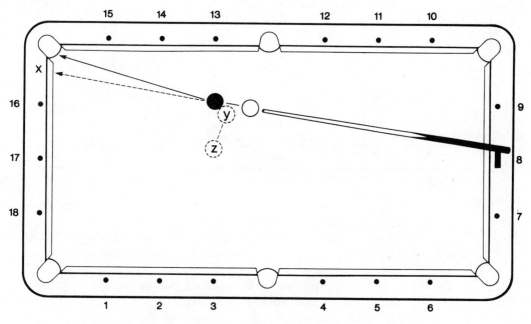

You may say: "The difference is only a few inches." Those few inches can mean victory or defeat in pool, as you will discover later.

Note: In applying left English in the above diagram, we said: "Strike the cue ball at 7:30 o'clock." The reader may well ask: "Why not strike the cue ball at 9:00 o'clock. Would that not apply *more* left English?"

The answer is "Yes." However, we have explained that *we use throw to minimize the movement of the cue ball.* At 7:30 o'clock, we add a little draw to the left English, which helps stop the cue ball.

The subject of English, as seen by a physicist, is far more complicated than the explanations given in this book, going deeply into vectors of angular momentum, precession, and the various coefficients of friction. The player will get the results he wants if he accepts the simplified explanation given in this book.

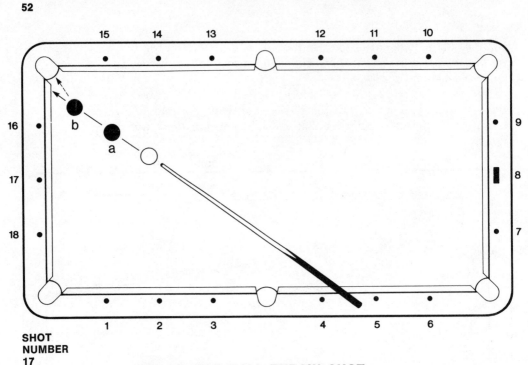

**SHOT
NUMBER
17**

THE DOUBLE BALL THROW SHOT
In the Single Ball Throw Shot (No. 16), we had just one object ball. When the cue ball transferred English to that one ball, we were through.

Here, however, we must influence two balls. *And notice that the two balls and the cue ball are all directly in line with the "X" on the cushion.*

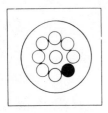

Strike the cue ball softly, putting on 4:30 *right* English—the opposite of what was used in Shot No. 16. Here is the scenario:

1. The 4:30 right English puts right English on the cue ball.

2. The cue ball, in turn, puts left English on ball "A".

3. Ball "A", in turn, puts right English on ball "B".

4. Ball "B" veers *right* into the pocket.

Again, as in the previous shot, you will control the cue ball.

Note: As we explained in Shot No. 16, the definitions of English given in this book would not meet the definitions of an experimental physicist. However, accept them for what they are, the age-old rules of thumb.
Nevertheless, do not think you can transfer spin down a long chain of balls. It is impossible.

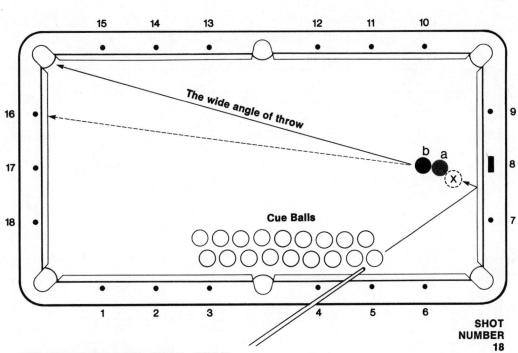

SHOT
NUMBER
18

OFF-THE-CUSHION PUSH SHOT

Above, we have a profusion of white cue balls to show that this beautiful shot can be made from many different positions.

Whichever cue ball you select, shoot it to come off the cushion into position "X", hitting ball "A" on the left, so that it will push right English on ball "B", and throw it into your pocket. (Imagine that you were shooting directly at ball "A", without having to ricochet off the cushion).

Notice how wide the angle of throw can be, when the thrown ball travels the entire length of the table. It is the width between two of the diamonds!

Hit softly enough so that maximum push will be put on ball "A".

Use a center shot, and remember! *You put no English on the cue ball. The English is put on the cue ball by the cushion; for the cue ball spins off with a twist.*

In the next shot, however, it is impossible to come off the cushion at an angle. Shoot at 7:30 o'clock, *putting strong left English on the cue ball itself.* Here the English on the cue ball brings the cue ball off the cushion at the proper angle. (p. 54, top)

There is still another variation, where even English on the cue ball will not help, and you have to carom off two cushions. Any shot from cue ball to object ball can usually be made with a carom from one cushion (or two, or three!). (p. 54, bottom)

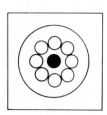

Experiment! These shots are not as difficult at they may seem.*

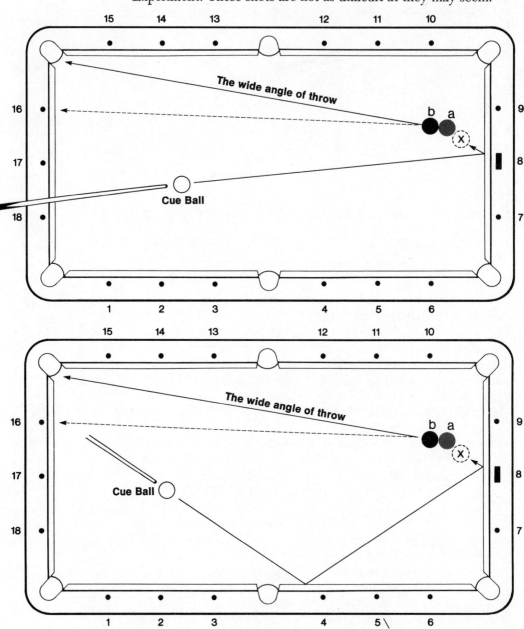

* As you go through this book, please keep in mind that we do not expect you to run into *the exact shot* in any given game. Every pool shot
differs from every other pool shot in some way; but if you understand the
principles, and try each shot that we give you, as your skill increases
your eye, arm, and brain will automatically adjust.

RUNNING ENGLISH vs. REVERSE ENGLISH
(Also known as "Natural" vs. "Unnatural" English)

On page 44, we put down every aspect of English except one —the effect of English as the spinning cue ball hits the cushion.

There are two kinds of "cushion English":

1. Running English, which adds speed to the cue ball, and widens the angle after the ball hits the cushion.

2. Reverse English, which cuts down the speed of the cue ball and narrows, or "closes", the angle.

How can you tell which is which?

Simply drop a line, in your mind's eye *from the cue ball* to the side of the table toward which you are shooting. If you are going to shoot to the right of this line, right English = running English. If you are going to shoot to the left of this line, left English = running English.

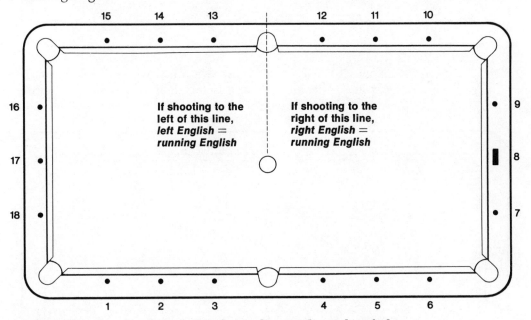

Consider the shot below. We have shot to the right of this imaginary line, so we have struck the cue ball at 3:00 o'clock, or right English. We say that this is running English because the spin of the ball "runs with the cushion," i.e., the ball is spinning so that it rolls smoothly off, speeds up, and "opens" the angle from which it leaves the cushion.

Had we shot to the left of our imaginary line, we would have shot at 9:00 o'clock, using left English, but again—we would be using "Running English."

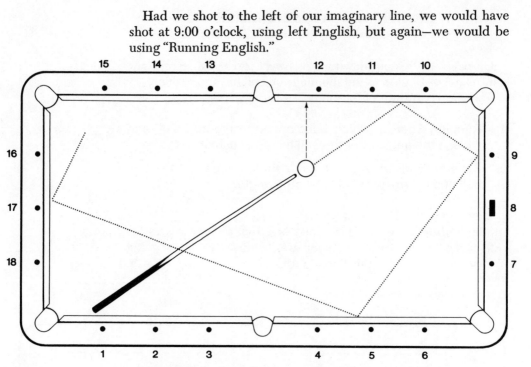

Now let's look at this same shot when we violate our "imaginary line" principle. We shot to the right, but used left English, or reverse English:

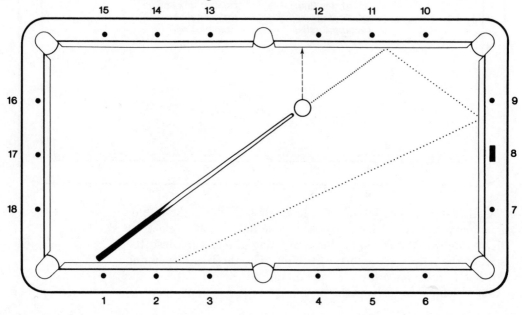

The ball is no longer running with the cushion. It is spinning in the opposite direction from which it is rolling. And notice the astounding difference! The angle of rebound is much narrower. Notice another thing! *Both shots were made at the same speed, and the reverse English slowed down the ball!*

There is one other thing to keep in mind when you practice the two Englishes: When you bank a ball around the table, *if it hits the first cushion with running English, it hits every adjoining cushion with running English.* In other words, if the ball leaves the first cushion with an open angle, it leaves every *adjoining* cushion with an open angle.

The key word here is "adjoining." If a ball with running English goes to the *opposite* cushion, it hits the cushion at such an angle that what *was* running English is now, suddenly, reverse.

Think about this until you understand it very clearly, for this is an important part of position play.

What happens when a ball with reverse English hits *adjoining* cushions? In this case the ball is not spinning in the direction that you are shooting, i.e., is spinning in the opposite direction from its line of flight. Because of cushion friction, this spin is reduced with each cushion that you hit, until finally the opposite spin is induced, and reverse English actually turns into running English! You generally cannot go more than two cushions before this transformation takes place.

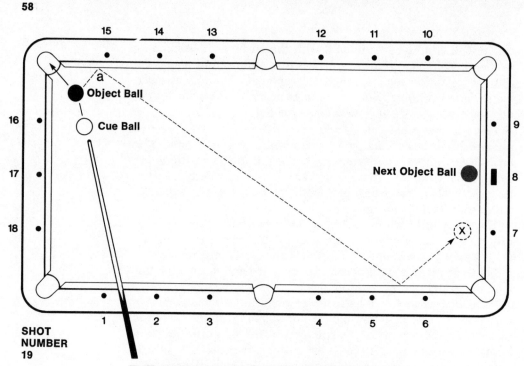

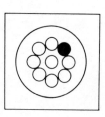

SHOT
NUMBER
19

THE RUNNING ENGLISH POSITION SHOT

Here we have a rather simple cut of the object ball into the corner pocket. However, *we want our cue ball to come down the full length of the table, and take up position for that second object ball.* Two pages ago, we could not have visualized this shot.

But now!

We cut the first object ball into the pocket using right English.*

This is "running English," so that our cue ball "runs with the cushion." To do this we strike the cue ball at 1:30 o'clock, and have the pleasure of watching the cue ball roll down the table into approximately position "X". The angle "a" is an *open* angle.

It turns out not to have been a difficult shot at all!

---

* When cutting a ball, and at the same time using English, the point of contact (reread shot No. 1) is slightly different on the ball. In this case the yawning pocket is so close that this may be ignored.
See Shot No. 26, the Cut Shot with English.

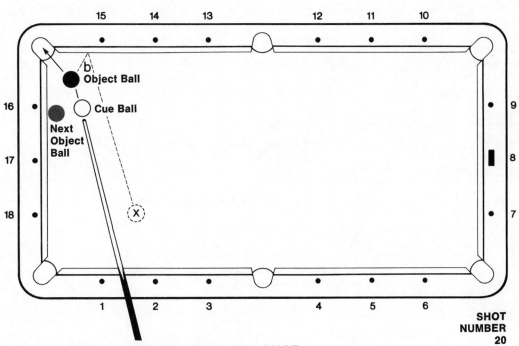

SHOT
NUMBER
20

THE REVERSE ENGLISH POSITION SHOT

Here again, we have a rather simple cut of the object ball into the corner pocket. However, our second object ball is only a few inches away. If the cue ball rolls down the length of the table, we are lost.

What do we do?

In this case we cut the object ball into the pocket using left English. This is not running English, but reverse English. So we strike the cue ball at 10:30 o'clock. What a difference from Shot No. 19! Angle "b" is *closed*. The cue ball comes almost straight back with a braking action which slows it down, right at "X".

Indeed, we are now playing position!

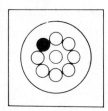

Note: In the section on Running English vs. Reverse English (page 55), if you were confused on open and closed angles, simply study Shots No. 19 and 20.

In Shot No. 19 the running English gave an open angle which carried the cue ball the length of the table. In Shot No. 20, the angle was so much more closed that the cue ball came almost directly back at the shooter.

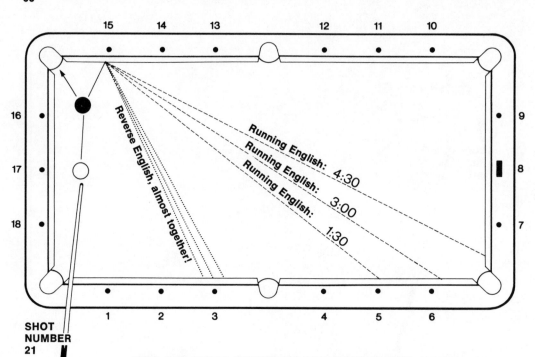

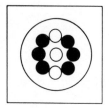

SHOT
NUMBER
21

THE RUNNING-REVERSE ENGLISH BASIC POSITION SHOT
No. 1

Is there a basic pattern for underlying this use of running and reverse English for position? The answer is "Yes"! Let us set up two more balls, this time in a slightly different position, and try *all the running English shots* (1:30, 3:00, and 4:30 o'clock) and *all the reverse English shots* (10:30, 9:00, and 7:30 o'clock).

Notice!

All of the reverse English shots, thanks to that closed angle, come back to within a few inches of the same diamond! All of the running English shots, because of their more open angles, fan out over the table!

No one who sets up this experiment should ever be at a loss, when playing position, on whether to use running or reverse English.

Set up the position. Use a medium stroke, then a soft stroke, then a hard stroke. Speed, you will discover, changes the angles somewhat, but the basic pattern remains the same.

Remember, too, that you can turn this pattern on it's side.

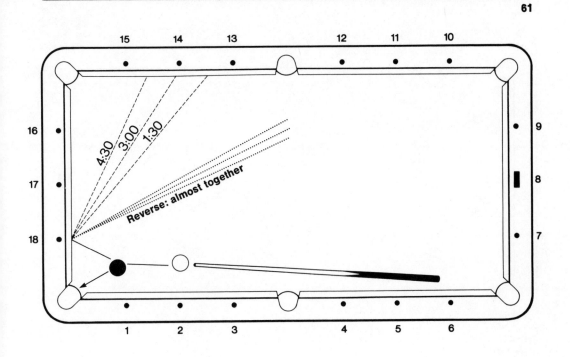

These are the same identical lines, except that you are now shoot-ing to the head of the table. In a textbook we always see the table from one side only. It pays to turn all of these shots in your mind's eye, or in practice, for you will be shooting from all sides of the table.

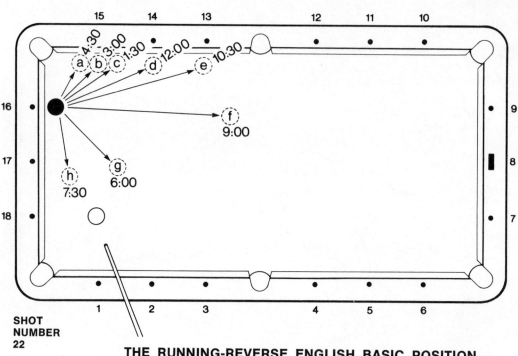

SHOT
NUMBER
22

THE RUNNING-REVERSE ENGLISH BASIC POSITION SHOT
No. 2

What happens in the above case where the cue ball is thrown immediately into the cushion? (In this shot, put the object ball ¼ inch from the cushion.)

Without attempting to trace out each shot, which would make one of the world's most confusing diagrams, we give above the end result. *Once again, it is a question of open or closed angles.*

When you put running English on the cue ball (in this case, right English), the open angles take the cue ball to "A", "B", and "C". 12:00 follow takes the cue ball to "D". Reverse English closes the angles and pulls the cue ball out to "E" and "F". A 6:00 o'clock Draw Shot brings it to "G", and a 7:30 Draw Shot to "H".*

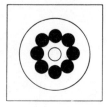

Study this closely. You will have similar shots many thousands of times.

---

* You strike the cue ball at 6:00 o'clock to draw it—or at 7:30 or 4:30, when you want draw with a bit of English. However, do not think merely hitting the cue ball will draw it. Reread Shot No. 7.
Draw is a very special technique with the cue.

Below is a chart of the same shot reversed, where the running English is left English.

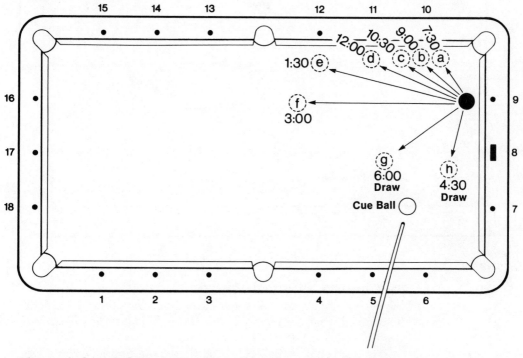

Thorough knowledge of this chart (like the one before) will save you thousands of times. Practice it with balls at different speeds, and in slightly different positions.

The positioning skill will then begin to become automatic.

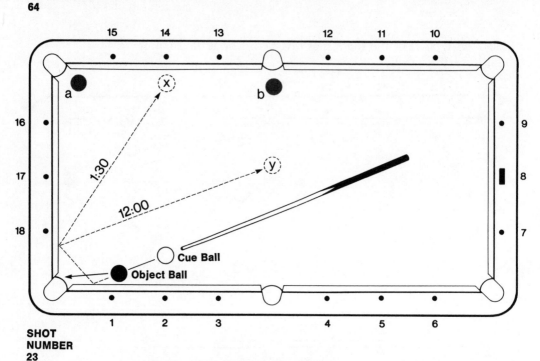

**SHOT
NUMBER
23**

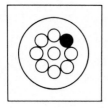

THE SHOOT THROUGH SHOT

In the previous shot we mentioned "shooting through" a ball. This means that *the cue ball rolls through where the object ball used to be.*

It is often an essential technique for getting position. To understand it precisely, put the object ball ½ inch off the diamond. Put the cue ball 2 inches off the next diamond.

Now sink the object ball with 1:30 follow. The cue ball rolls through the position of the object ball, comes off of two cushions, and stops at "X", ready to sink ball "A". A center ball shot would never achieve this position.

Try the same shot, using 12:00 o'clock follow. Now the cue ball stops at "Y", ready to sink ball "A" or "B".

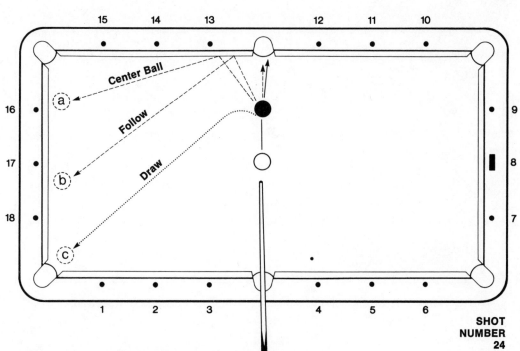

THE SIDE POCKET CHEAT-THE-POCKET SHOT

In Shot No. 4 we described the "cheat-the-pocket" technique. Since the pocket is wider than the ball,* don't shoot the object ball straight in. Hit it at a slight angle, so that we get position on the cue ball.

Here we cut the object ball slightly to the left, using 6:00 o'clock draw, 12:00 follow, and center ball. Use a medium speed.

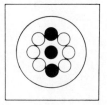

Our cue ball goes to "A", "B", or "C"—and, depending on our speed, can be at any position on any of these lines, or even beyond!

We can reverse the shot above, of course, by cheating the pocket on the opposite side.

Notice the curve put on by the draw!

* The side pocket is actually wider that a corner pocket—5⅜ minimum to 5⅝ maximum, whereas the corner pocket is only 4⅞ minimum to 5⅛ maximum.

The ball is only 2¼ inches in diameter, so we have ample room for cheating.

Keep in mind that in these diagrams we are using an *enormously enlarged ball.*

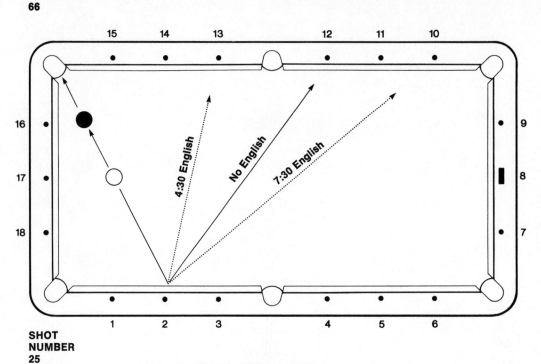

SHOT
NUMBER
25

THE REVERSE DRAW SHOT

Just as we use English to make the cue ball come off the rail in various ways, so we can use draw. What is more, we can use draw to give us running English or reverse English.

Sink the object ball, using powerful draw. The cue ball will whip to the rail, *hitting it with the same English we applied!* If we strike the cue ball with 4:30 draw, it hits the rail with 4:30 spin. If we use 7:30 draw, it hits the rail with 7:30. *It is exactly the same as walking to the opposite side of the table, striking the cue ball with the cue, and shooting it from the other side with 4:30 or 7:30 English!*

Many players get this backward. Simply because it is a draw, they think that right English comes back as left, and left English comes back as right.

Not so.

If, from the other side of the table, 7:30 is running English (which it is), so it is if you draw with 7:30 English.

If confused, walk around the table and pick your English. Then, come back and draw with it!

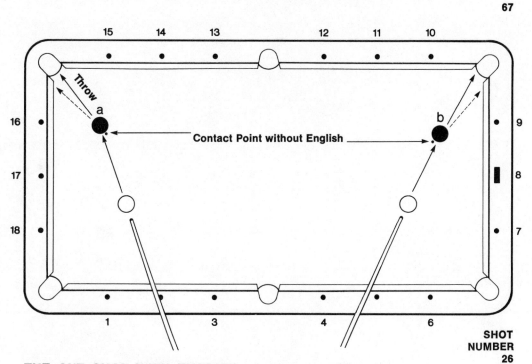

Contact Point without English

SHOT
NUMBER
26

THE CUT SHOT WITH ENGLISH

In Shot No. 1 we discussed the point of contact, the exact point at which the cue ball must strike the object ball to sink a shot.

Now, however, in many of our previous shots we have been adding English to play position.

And English adds throw!

To compensate for the throw, we must move the point of contact either to the right or left, or the ball will go into the cushion instead of the pocket.

Here is the rule: *Move the point of contact in the direction of the throw.*

In this example let us assume that we want to put right English on our cue ball to get a certain position. This will throw ball "A" to the left. So we shoot just to the left of our previous contact point, which compensates for this.

On ball "B" we are using left English to get position. This throws ball "B" to the right. So we shoot just to the right of our previous contact point, and again we compensate.

Move the point of contact in the direction of the throw!

How far do you move it? We can only say again: Practice! Practice! Practice!

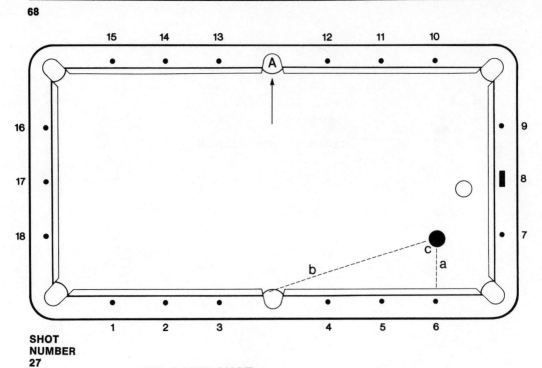

SHOT
NUMBER
27

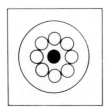

THE BANK SHOT

Let us assume that you have only one way to sink the ball above. You must bank it off the cushion, so that it rolls acros the table into the side pocket, "A".

"Where," you wonder, "must the cue ball hit the cushion?"

There is a simple way to find out. In your mind's eye, drop a line ("a") from the object ball to the cushion, and another line ("b") to the pocket *across from the pocket* in which you plan to sink your ball (A). *If you can find the exact center of this angle ("c"), you will know the spot.*

Unfortunately, it is hard to do this accurately. Hence the following trick, which seems complicated, but is in reality quite simple:

Lay your cue stick down on the table, *reaching from where line "a" touched the cushion to the pocket in which you wish to sink the ball.* It crosses line "b" at "x".

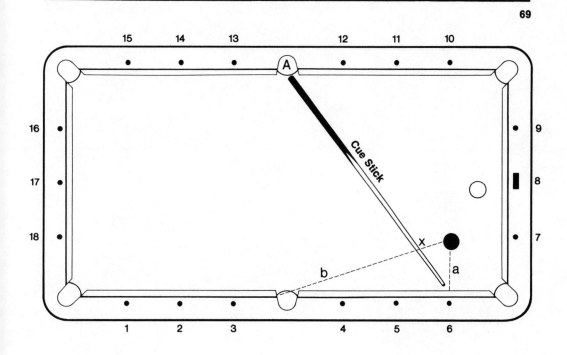

Now, drop a line in your mind's eye down from "x" to the cushion—and that's the spot to which you shoot the object ball (arrow). You come out with this shot:

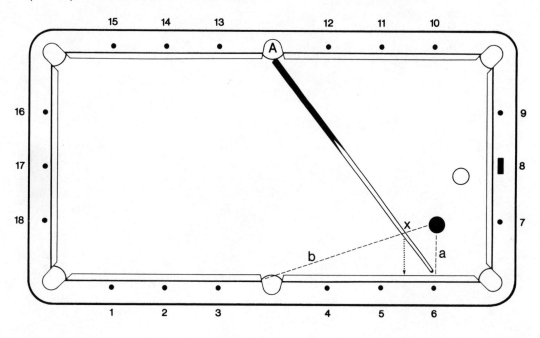

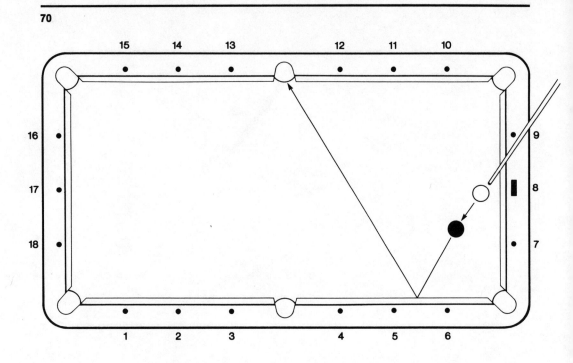

This is not as complicated as it seems. With a half-hour practice, holding the cue stick over the balls a few inches from the cloth, you can draw the lines with your eyes and come up with the exact spot.

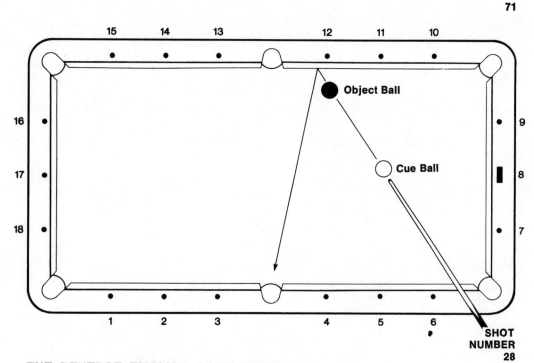

THE REVERSE ENGLISH BANK SHOT

Now and then (review Shot No. 27), even when you know the spot where your object ball must hit the cushion, you will find it impossible to shoot it. The cue ball, after it hits, may be so close to the cushion that the object ball will rebound into the cue ball. This ruins the shot.

Above is just such a case. The object ball is one ball's distance from diamond No. 12, and the cue ball is on the spot.*

What is the solution?

Strike the cue ball at 7:30 o'clock, using a moderate stroke to stop the cue ball. *This low, left English will put right English, or reverse English, on the object ball.** (Think of it as putting the object ball on the spot, and striking it with the cue at 4:30 o'clock.) This reverse English shortens the angle at which the object ball banks off the cushion, so that it rolls into the side pocket without interference from the cue ball.

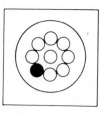

---

* See official diagram on page 173 for placement of spots.

* See "Running English vs. Reverse English", page 55.

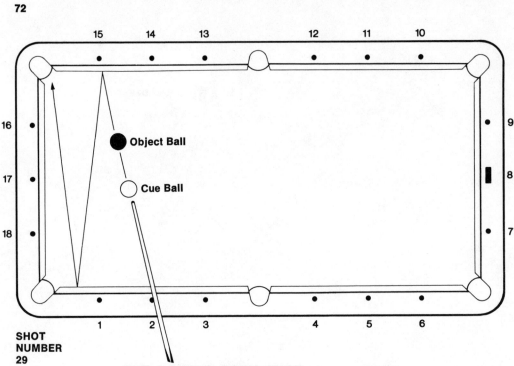

SHOT NUMBER 29

THE DOUBLE BANK SHOT

Sometimes, even when you have a one-shot bank into some pocket, you may wish to try for a double bank *which is the only way you can make another pocket*. You may want to hold the cue ball in a certain position, or you may be playing the game "One Pocket," in which case you can only sink the ball in one specific pocket. Any number of situations may arise.

The only solution is to bank off two cushions. No book can teach you this shot. It is purely a judgment shot, and it calls for practice to train the eye.

Mark the position of two balls with chalk. Shoot until you sink the ball, and market the two cushions where the object ball must hit. Then, repeat it until you train your eye. Next try a different position for the balls. Before long you will feel the instinct beginning to come from your "eye, arm and brain computer"—which is the secret of excellence in all pool.

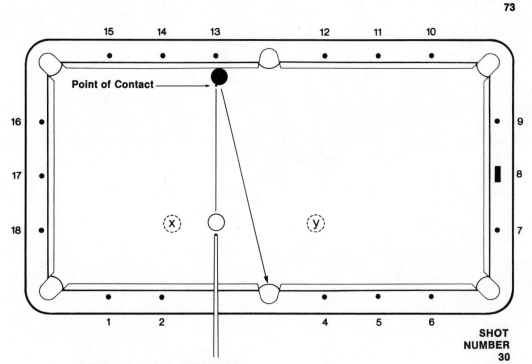

SHOT NUMBER 30

THE IN LINE FROZEN BANK SHOT

Can a ball frozen against the cushion be banked across the table, *when the cue ball is directly in front of the object ball?*

The answer is "Yes."

In the above position, shoot to cut the cue ball exactly in half. The simplest way to do this is to aim your cue stick through the center of the cue ball, at the left edge of the object ball.

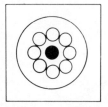

Shoot hard to deflect the cue ball out of the way. If you shoot too softly, you are in peril of a double kiss, i.e., the object ball will spring back off the cushion and hit the cue ball a second time.

Pause now, consider carefully what we are going to say:

1. In the exact position above, if you move your cue ball to "X", the shot *looks* easier, but—it's impossible! When you hit that point of contact, you get a double kiss.

2. If you move your cue ball to "Y", you can still make the shot! For you can still reach that point of contact, and *with less chance of a double kiss!*

3. If you move cue ball and object ball to the left (but still in line), with each move you will hit less and less of the object ball, to widen the angle. And obviously, too far to the left the shot becomes impossible.

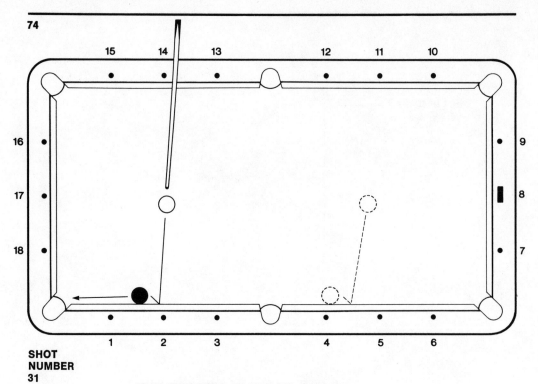

THE FROZEN CUSHION SHOT
No. 1

Here is a shot that comes up with amazing frequency. The object ball is frozen against the cushion, and the cue ball faces it at a very steep angle.

Most players try to "feather" the object ball, i.e., hit with the slimmest possible cut. This is tremendously difficult. *However, it is quite easy to sink the shot—by missing it!*

Shoot into the cushion as close as possible to the object ball, *without touching it*. Use right English at 4:30 o'clock. The cue ball will rebound from the cushion, hit the object ball in the center, and roll it into the pocket. Shoot slowly enough to get good English.

With a little practice, you can make this shot when the object ball is as far away as diamond Nos. 4 and 5!

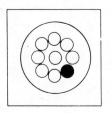

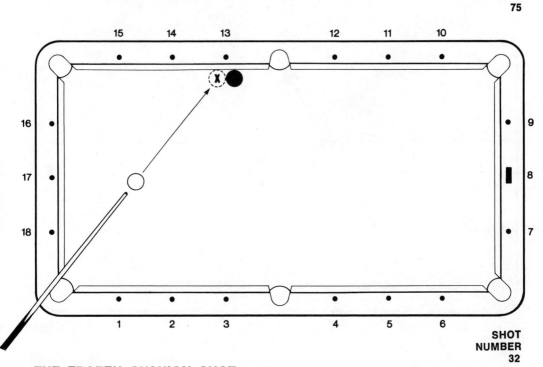

SHOT
NUMBER
32

THE FROZEN CUSHION SHOT
No. 2

Here again (as in Shot No. 31) the object ball is frozen against the cushion. However, the angle of the cue ball is not as extreme.

This shot, which comes up thousands of times, should be shot without English so that *the cue ball hits the object ball and the cushion at the same time.*

It must, in other words, come into the same position as the ghost ball "X".

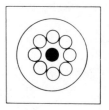

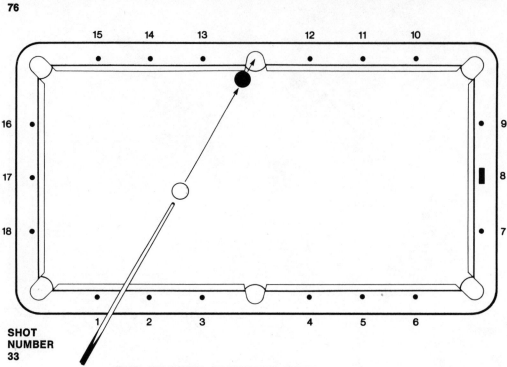

**SHOT
NUMBER
33**

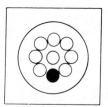

THE FROZEN CUSHION SHOT
No. 3

Here the object ball is not only frozen against the cushion, but is so overhanging the pocket that no seemingly logical shot can sink it into the side pocket. A soft shot won't put it in; it can't be cut in, or rolled in. It's just stuck there.

It's one of the easiest shots in pool!

Hit the cut ball *hard* at 6:00 o'clock—and hit the object ball in dead center. The force of the shot compresses the cushion as though it were not there, and the ball goes almost magically into the side pocket.

Similar shots can be made in the corner pockets.

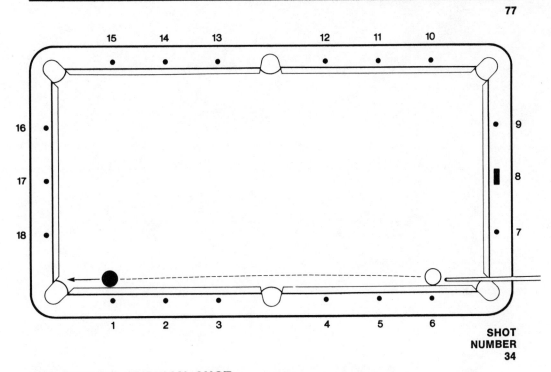

SHOT
NUMBER
34

THE FROZEN CUSHION SHOT
No. 4

This is also a shot which comes up amazingly often. It is usually disastrous, for the cue ball hits one of the "horns" of the side pocket and veers out into the table.

Depending on whether you are shooting from right to left or vice-versa, use 4:30 or 7:30 o'clock English. *Simply make sure that the English is on the side of the ball closest to the cushion.*

The dotted line (a bit exaggerated) shows that the cue ball comes out from the cushion, misses the side pocket, and then the English pulls it back in to make the other ball.

Shoot softly! Shoot just hard enough to sink the other ball. Otherwise, your cue ball will follow the object ball into the pocket.

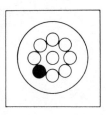

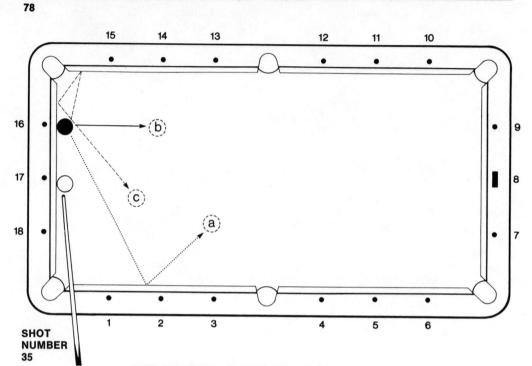

SHOT
NUMBER
35

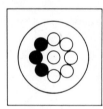

THE FROZEN CUSHION SHOT
No. 5

Here again the cue ball and the object ball are frozen against the same cushion, but the problem is a different one:

If we shoot the object ball straight in, the cue ball will stay on the rail. *How do we get the cue ball off the rail, to get position on some other ball?*

There are three ways to do it:

1. *Shooting slightly inward* (notice the angle of the cue!) strike the cue ball at 7:30 o'clock. This draw forces the cue ball to position "A".

2. Shooting slightly inward, strike the cue ball at 9:00 o'clock. The cue ball will come straight out to position "B".

3. Shooting slightly inward again, strike the cue ball at 10:30 o'clock. The cue ball will come off two cushions to position "C".*

The draw shot, which is the easiest, is the most used. However, since this shot comes up in game after game, it is a "must" on your list of secret weapons. *It is a positional shot known to very few players.*

---

* On the opposite cushion, of course, all these shots would be reversed.

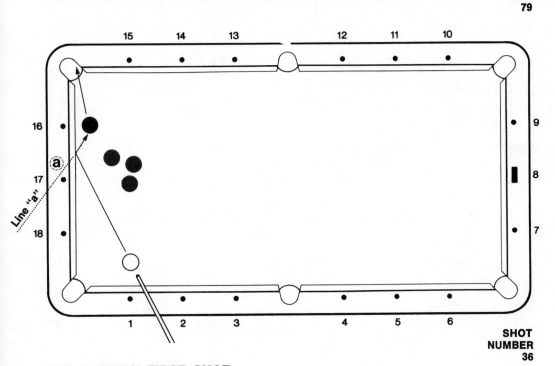

SHOT
NUMBER
36

THE CUSHION FIRST SHOT
No. 1

Here there is no way that the cue ball can make a direct shot on the object ball. The solution is to come off the cushion first, and *carom into the object ball as though you were shooting the cue ball down line "a".*

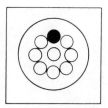

To understand this shot exactly, put the object ball ½ inch off diamond No. 16, and the cue ball ½ diamond off diamond No. 1. Hit the cushion ¾ of a ball ahead of the object ball.

Shoot at 12:00 o'clock English, with a soft stroke.

Set such shots up at different distances and different angles. Shoot them over and over! Feed them into that "eye, arm and brain computer." *For even when you can hit the object ball directly, you often need these Cushion First shots for position.*

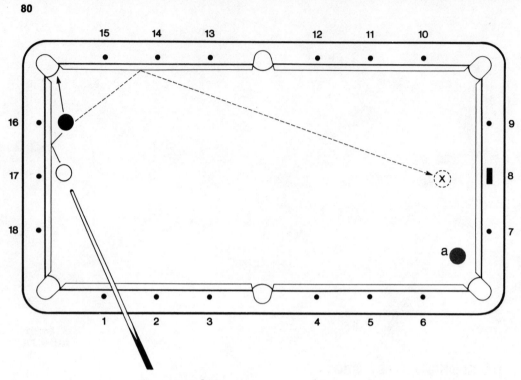

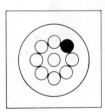

For example:

Here (the balls are 1 inch off the two diamonds) it is easy to sink the object ball directly. However, we want to come down the table to take position on ball "A". So we shoot cushion-first at 1:30 o'clock, to get running English—and presto! We roll down to "X".

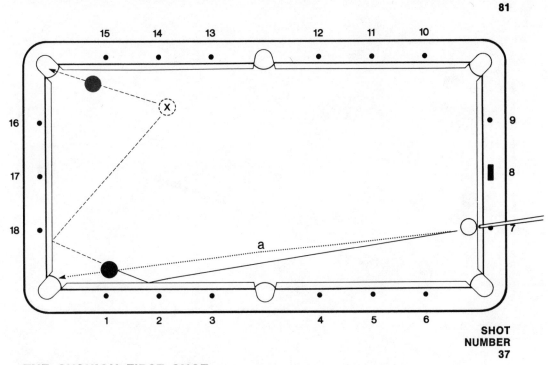

THE CUSHION FIRST SHOT
No. 2

Here we have a straight shot into the corner pocket, as shown by the dotted line. We wish to play position, however, and have our cue ball stop at "X". However, there are two things against us: (1) The cue ball is frozen against the cushion, so we must strike the cue ball at 12:00 o'clock, which is a follow shot, and the cue ball may follow the object ball into the pocket; (2) After we sink the object ball, there is no way of getting to "X".

The solution?

Make a Cushion First Shot!

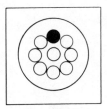

To practice this, put the object ball off diamond No. 1 as shown. Freeze the cue ball against diamond No. 7. Hit the cushion first, as shown. The cue ball will carom off diamond No. 18, and roll over to "X".

There are thousands of variants of this shot. Move the cue ball straight down line "a" to get a wide number, and then try varying line "a".

The shot in the diagram is an easy shot. You should succeed in your first three or four tries. In fact, many fine players find it easier than sinking the object ball with a straight shot.

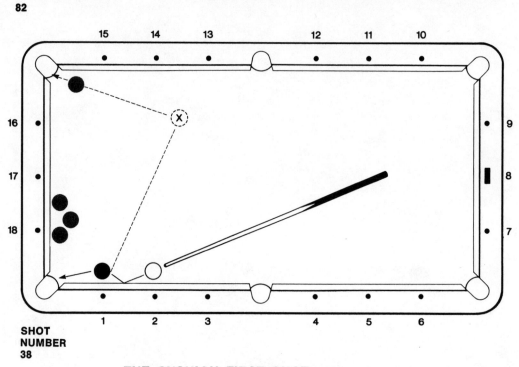

**SHOT
NUMBER
38**

THE CUSHION FIRST SHOT
No. 3

This shot has the same theory at Shot No. 37, except that we can't come off the second cushion because of other balls.

To practice it, put the cue ball and the object ball ½ inch from the two diamonds.

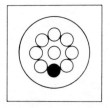

Make a Cushion First shot, using draw at 6:00 o'clock. Without reaching the second rail, you will roll across the table to "X".

There will be thousands of times when the second cushion is blocked to you, and you will be lost without knowing this very *unobvious* draw shot.

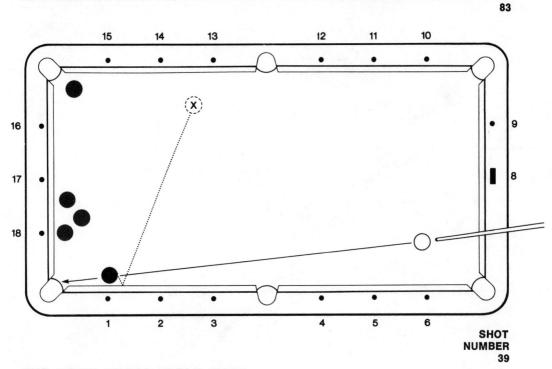

THE DRAW CROSS TABLE SHOT

This is the same shot as No. 37, except that we are not on the cushion, and again (as in Shot No. 38) have those "interference balls."

Since a pool player should have every weapon in his arsenal, let's now cross the table with draw.

Stroke the cue ball at 6:00 o'clock. Cheat the pocket slightly (see Shot No. 4) so that you cut the shot just enough to throw the cue ball into the cushion. Sink the object ball. The cue ball will then move across the table to "X".

This "deflect into the cushion with draw" is a technique that you will use again and again and again!

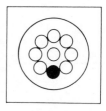

Note: It is difficult, in diagrams using enlarged balls, to show subtleties in position. Keep in mind (see Shot No. 37) that the object ball must be placed ½ inch from diamond No. 1, so that what seems in the diagram to be a straight-in shot *is not straight in.* Hence the deflection of the cue ball into the cushion.

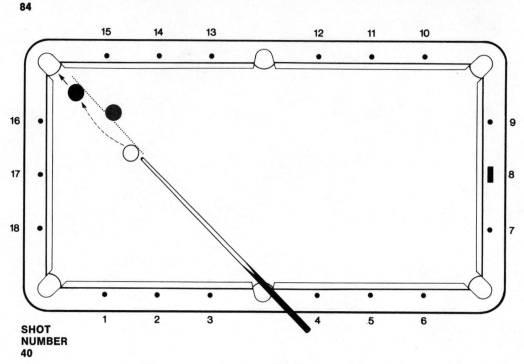

SHOT
NUMBER
40

THE CURVED BALL SHOT

If you tried to sink the object ball here, the cue ball would carom off the gray ball, for the gray ball intrudes on the path of the cue ball about ⅛ inch. You can see it peeping over the line of shot.

An impossible shot? No! It can be mastered in about thirty minutes, and it's a secret weapon in the pool shooter's arsenal; for most players do not know it, and you run into it thousands of times!

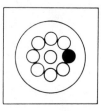

Elevate the butt of the cue to a 45° angle. Shoot the cue ball *downwards* at 3:00 o'clock. The cue ball will swerve first to the left, just enough to miss the gray ball, and then swerve to the right to sink the object ball!

Here is a reverse version. (opposite, top)

Put the cue ball one ball's width from diamond No. 9. Put the object ball 1½ inches from diamond No. 7. Again, elevate the butt of the cue to a 45° angle, shoot downwards (this time at 9:00 o'clock)—shooting the cue ball as close as possible to the gray ball. Presto!

Both of these are very short shots. Here the same magic is used over a longer distance. (opposite, bottom)

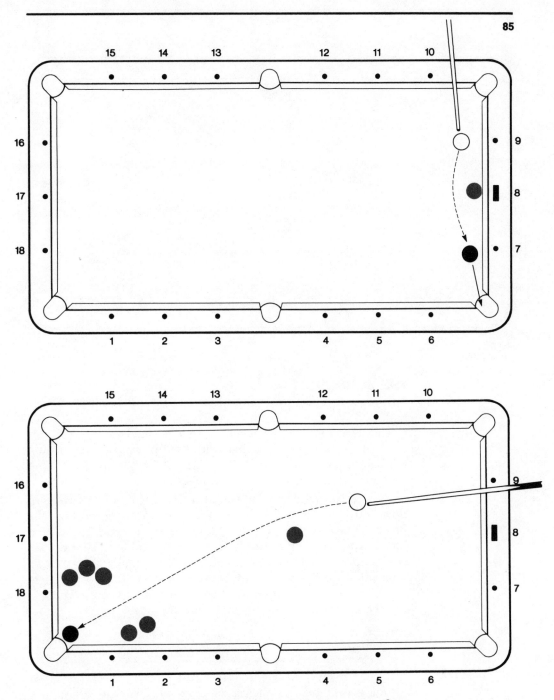

Keep in mind that in every case you must have a very firm
control over the cue. You must shoot downward with authority,
yet softly enough so that the English will have maximum "take."

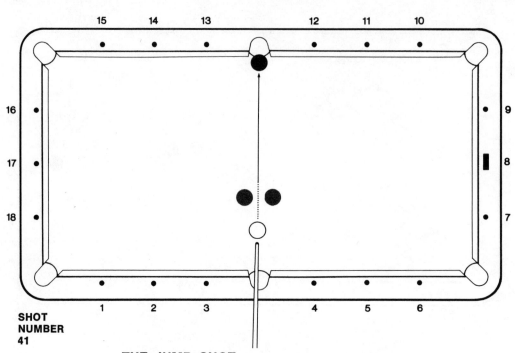

SHOT
NUMBER
41

THE JUMP SHOT

Is it legal to make the cue ball take to the air to clear another ball?

The answer is "Yes!"—depending on how you do it.

If you dig *under* the cue ball with the tip of your cue, causing the ball to jump, it is a foul. But *if you strike the cue ball in the center or above center, the jump is legal.**

Elevate the butt of your cue at a 45° angle, and strike *hard* downward on the cue ball. Hit one cue tip above center. The ball will take to the air with the greatest of ease. The dotted line shows where the cue ball leaves the table. The cue ball comes up just high enough to clear the horizontal axis of the two interfering balls, which are too close together to shoot through.

A side view of the jump would look like this, if you were looking at one of the interference balls from the side.

* The Billiard Congress of America's rule on jump shots reads: "If a player causes a ball to jump . . . deliberately, by elevating the butt end of the cue and striking the cue ball in the center or above center, the jump is legal. If, however, a player digs under the cue ball with the tip end of his cue, causing the ball to jump, the stroke is foul. Penalty: loss of one point."

The jump shot is most often used to clear a part of one ball, as below:

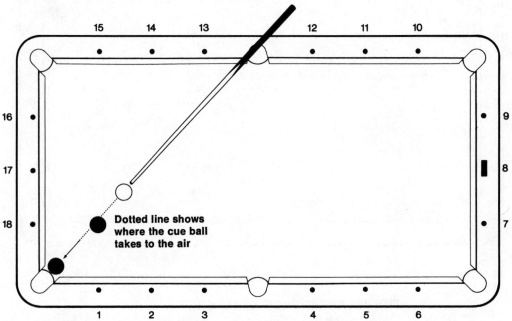

Dotted line shows where the cue ball takes to the air

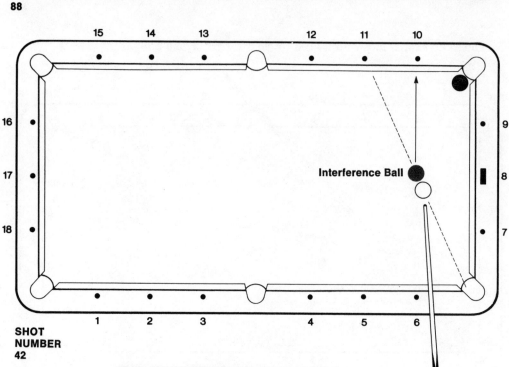

SHOT
NUMBER
42

THE INTERFERENCE BALL SHOT

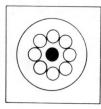

You want to shoot the cue ball to sink the object ball, but can't. The interference ball blocks the shot.

Draw a mental line *bisecting the cue ball and the interference ball and running into the cushion* (in this case diamond No. 11). Cut the distance in half, as indicated by the arrow (here it happens to be diamond No. 10).

Shoot the cue ball directly at this half-way point. The interference ball will be deflected out of the way, putting the cue ball on the proper course to sink the object ball.

Here again is a shot that will occur many thousands of times. Depending on the distance, use soft to medium speed.

Since this shot is really a carom shot,* let us pass on to Carom Shots, which are among the most critical shots in pool.

* (See Glossary, page 207) Carom Shot: When a cue ball glances off the object ball into a second (or third) ball. Also known as a "kiss".

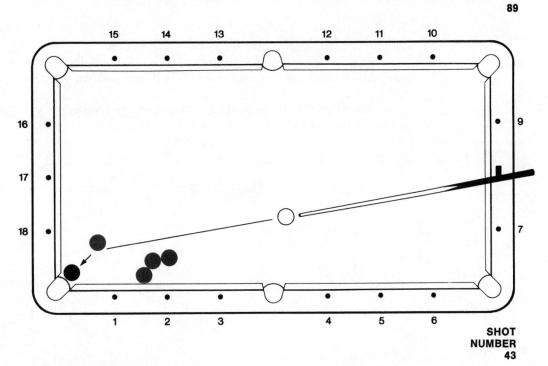

SHOT
NUMBER
43

THE CAROM SHOT

Thousands of times you will find that some obstruction prevents you from sinking a ball. In this case, it is the cluster of gray balls.

Or, *you may be forced to hit one specific ball first* (this can come up often in Nine Ball, or Rotation) before you sink a second ball.

And thousands of times the solution will be the Carom Shot. You will find that you can carom, or "kiss," off an intermediate ball.

The key question here is: "At what point do you hit the inter-mediate ball? What is the point of aim?"

There is a convenient formula which looks complicated but isn't. In fact, it is one of the easiest computations on the pool table:

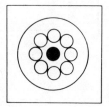

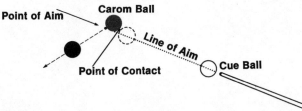

Draw a line through the center of the ball you wish to sink and the carom ball. (We are assuming here that the ball you wish to sink is in front of the pocket.) *Simply aim through your cue ball*

directly at the point of aim. You will hit the carom ball on the contact point, of course, due to the curvature of the balls. However, the cue ball will kiss off the carom ball, and sink the second ball.

Keep in mind that there are Carom Shots where you may wish to shoot an object ball into the carom ball. Witness:

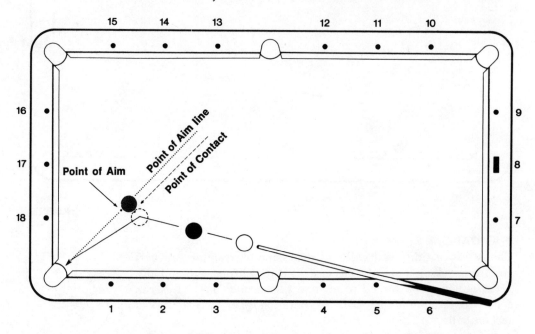

To establish your point of aim here, draw a line from the center of the pocket through the carom ball.

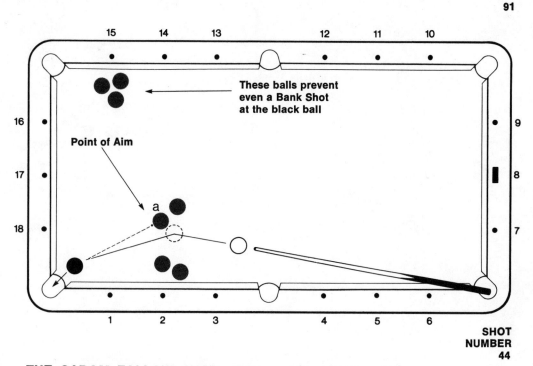

THE CAROM FOLLOW SHOT

The previous shot was a center ball shot, where the cue ball glances off the gray ball at a simple angle. Sometimes, however, the cue ball must *follow* the gray ball down the table.

For example, due to the obstruction balls, there is no way that the cue ball can hit ball "A", and sink the black ball, without a Carom Follow Shot.

Shoot at 12:00 o'clock.

Select your *point of aim* exactly as in Shot No. 43.

It is a much easier shot than it seems. The cue ball will roll serenely down to sink the black ball!

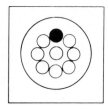

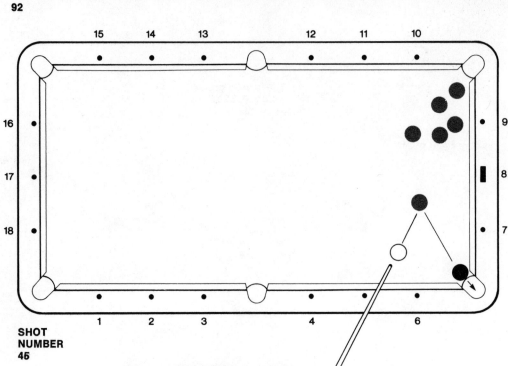

SHOT
NUMBER
45

THE CAROM DRAW SHOT

An eye-opener to many players!

Here the cue ball hits the gray ball, spins sharply backward at an acute angle, and click! The black ball drops in the pocket! It looks, as pool players say, like a "miracle shot."

The secret, of course, is draw. And the first question is: *"Is there a system whereby we can determine the point of aim (not point of contact) as effectively as we did in Shots No. 43 and 44?"*

The answer is "Yes." It is a different system, but it is equally simple.

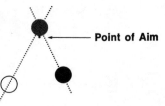

Point of Aim

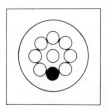

In your mind's eye, draw two lines connecting the center of the carom ball with the centers of the cue ball and the black ball. Split this angle in the middle, and you have the point of *aim.*

Simply aim through your cue ball at this point, keep your cue level, and shoot at 6:00 o'clock!

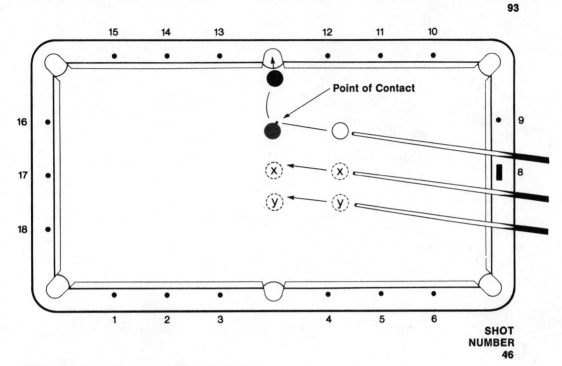

Point of Contact

SHOT
NUMBER
46

THE RIGHT ANGLE CAROM SHOT

Here the balls are at an exact right angle. Again, as in the previous shot, we split the angle to get our *point of aim.*

And again, we use a draw shot.

The cue ball, in hitting the object ball, *not only goes sideways but a bit forward.* As it does, the reverse bites in, and curves it back to the straight line, and—we sink the black ball!*

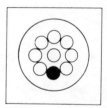

Practice this by moving the gray ball further away, to "X" and "Y". You will need more speed, but before long the exact speed will be coming out of your "eye, arm and brain computer"—and you will have added this fine shot to your repertoire.

---

* The same shot can be made with center ball, hitting the gray ball about ⅘ full. *The stroke must be much harder.* Some players, in perfecting the center ball version, prefer to add a little right English.

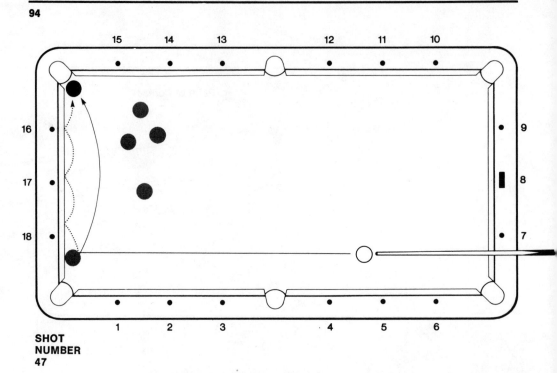

SHOT
NUMBER
47

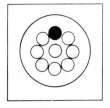

THE FROZEN BALL CAROM

Here the black object ball is so screened by interference balls that there is only one way to sink it. We must carom off the ball frozen against the cushion, so that the cue ball splits across the table.

A difficult shot? Well, it isn't easy, but you can add it to your repertoire once you have mastered the *speed* of the shot.

Hit ⅓ of the ball frozen against the cushion, using 12:00 o'clock follow. If you shoot too hard, as the cue ball caroms off the gray ball, it will have too much forward spin and will drive repeatedly into the rail (dotted line). You may miss the object ball. But if you shoot with a "just right" speed, your cue ball will follow the black arrow.

The same shot, with the cue ball at an oblique angle, can be made from the longer cushion:

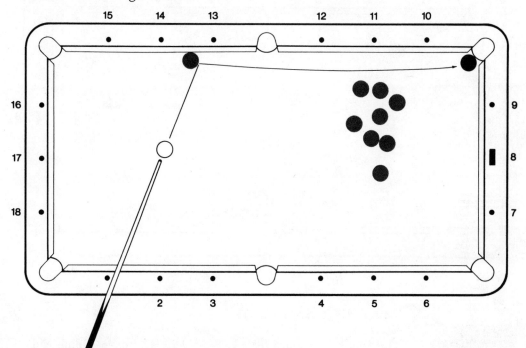

From all of these caroms, we progress naturally to the Ghost Ball Shots—wizardry, seeming magic at the pool table, and so easy (once you *see* them) you can hardly miss!

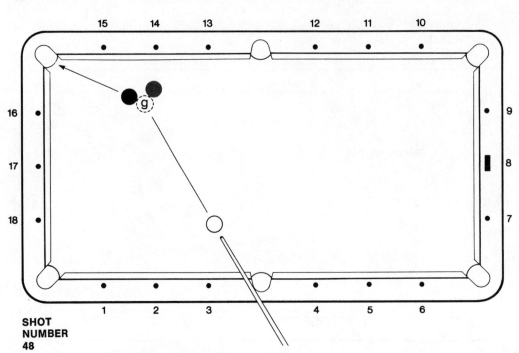

SHOT
NUMBER
48

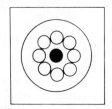

THE GHOST BALL SHOT
No. 1

This shot is a stunner! It looks like magic! Opponents blink when they see it! Some of the best players in the world don't know it—and yet it is one of the easiest shots in pool.

However, you must *see* it. You must recognize it, as it lies there hidden among many balls. Once you do—click! You can't miss.

Shoot the cue ball above, as indicated, at the gray object ball. When it reaches the ghost ball position (the round dotted line) you will find two of our old friends (Shot Nos. 12 and 13), except that we achieve it by caroming the cue ball off the gray ball:

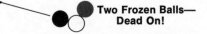

Two Frozen Balls—
Dead On!

The cue ball, of course, must approach the gray carom ball at a slight angle, to set the object ball in motion.

Here is the same shot, as encountered by Ray Martin in a recent tournament. The ghost ball is marked with a "G". The average player wouldn't have *seen* the opportunity. Ray knew that if he shot ball "A", it would propel ball "B" into the ghost ball slot, and ball "C" would roll automatically into the corner pocket. *But you must see the shot.* In many apparently random packs of balls you can find dozens of the shots in this book, providing that you can see the hidden pattern.

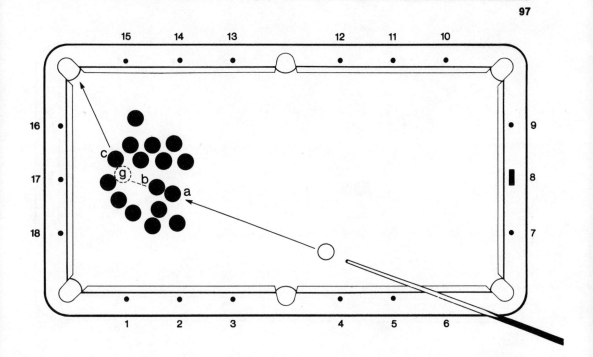

Here is still another version. Again, we have marked the ghost ball with a "G".

How easy! You strike the cue ball without any English. You simply have to move the cue ball into the ghost space!

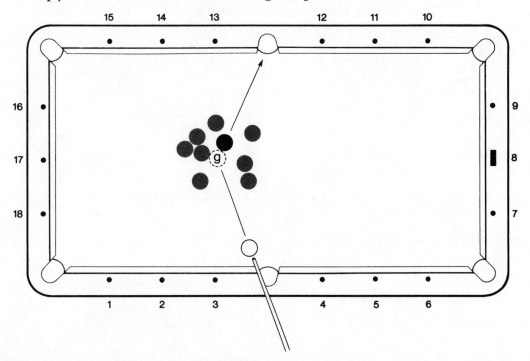

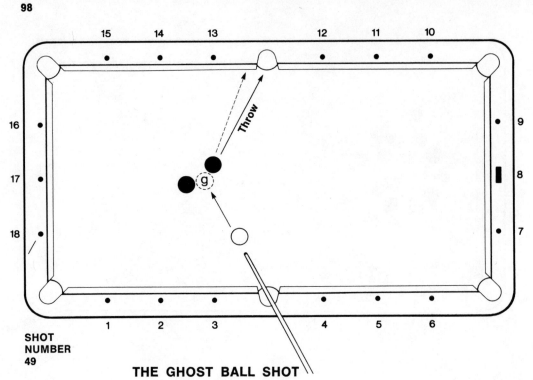

THE GHOST BALL SHOT
No. 2

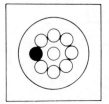

In all of the previous Ghost Ball Shots, the two balls, once aligned, were dead on. Here they are not, and a straight shot would simply roll the object ball into the cushion.

Shoot with left English—say 9:00 o'clock. This will put right English on the object ball, and throw it* to the right into the pocket.

The opposite, of course, would be done with right English.

* See page 44 on English, and Shot Nos. 14 through 18 on the subject of throw.

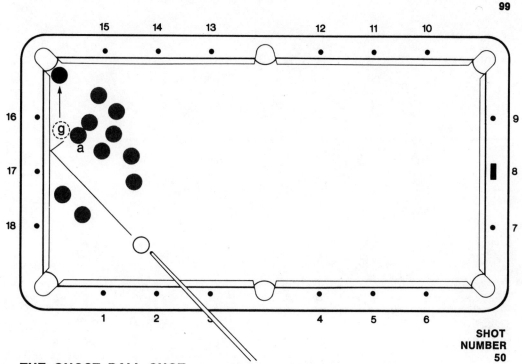

THE GHOST BALL SHOT
No. 3

Here, too, is a shot that occurs with great frequency *whenever
there is one ball near enough to the rail to set up a ghost ball
opportunity.*

In this case the ball near the rail, ball "A", must give about ⅛ of
an inch leeway on each side of the ghost ball.

Shoot to hit the rail first.

Let us repeat again: You must train yourself to *see inside a
cluster of balls the dozens of various shots in this book.*

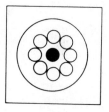

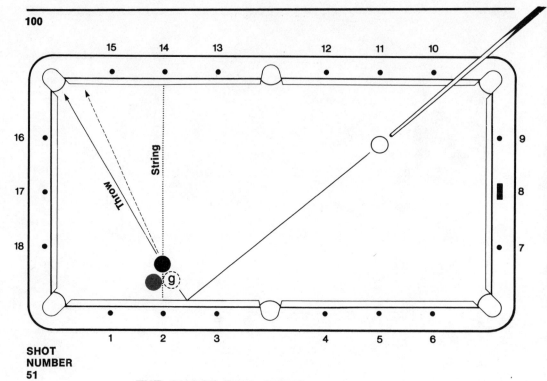

SHOT
NUMBER
51

THE GHOST BALL SHOT
No. 4

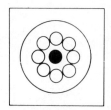

This is really a Backward Ghost Ball Shot. As you can see from the black arrow, once the cue ball has taken up the ghost ball's position at "G", the object ball will be shot to hit the cushion, for the line-up is not directly on the pocket.

The solution? It's built-in to the shot! The cue ball hits the rail first. This picks up right English, which in turn transmits left English to the object ball. The left English throws the object ball into the pocket.

To practice this shot, put the gray ball right on the edge of the string,* and the object ball ½ on the string, 1¼ inches from the gray ball. Put the cue ball in the corner of the rectangle formed by diamonds No. 9 and No. 11.

From the ghost ball shot it is only a step to the Nudge Shot—one of the prettiest and most valuable shots in pool.

---

* See official diagram on page 173 for placement of strings.

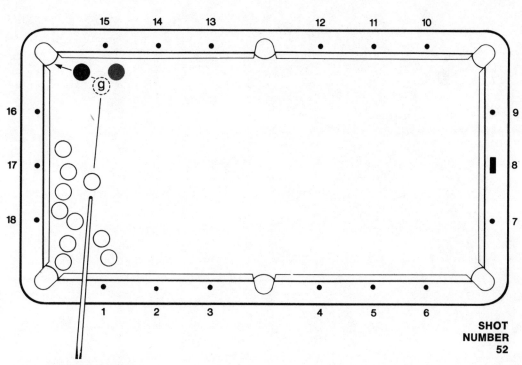

SHOT
NUMBER
52

THE NUDGE SHOT

Once you have mastered the Nudge Shot, it will become one of your secret weapons. Very few players know this shot. Let us give you some precise positions so that you can grasp the principles involved.

Set up the object ball and the gray ball ¼ inch off the cushion, on each side of diamond No. 15, so that one ball can go between them with ⅛ of an inch on each side.

Now shoot at 3:00 o'clock between the two balls, *without touching the object ball, and very thinly slicing the gray ball.* We have put a dotted circle to show you how a given cue ball should come in on the gray ball.

Result? The cue ball kisses off the gray ball, spins directly into the object ball, and sinks it in the pocket.

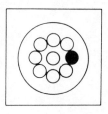

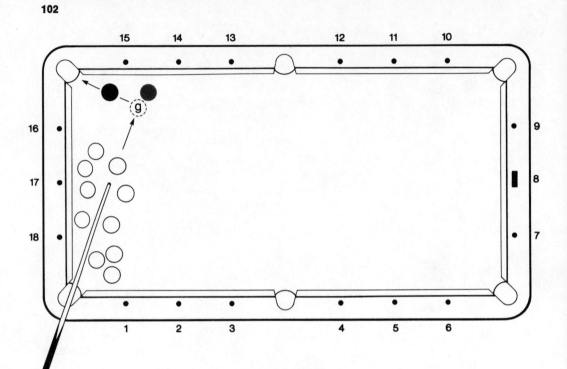

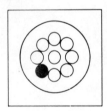

In the variant above, the balls are much more widely separated, with 1½ balls' distance between (slightly over 3⅛ inches). Now hit ½ of the gray ball, using 7:30 o'clock draw. Again, the object ball rolls into the pocket.

The Nudge Shot is first cousin, actually, to what we call the Carom Draw Shot (Shot No. 45).

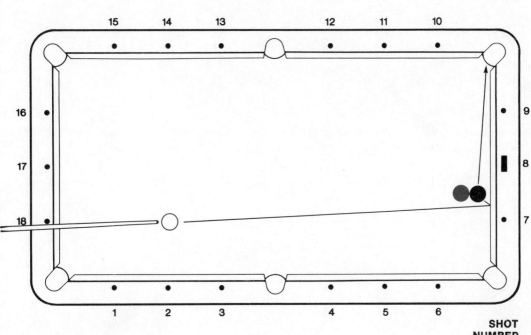

SHOT
NUMBER
53

THE RAIL KISS SHOT

This is another shot that smacks of magic, but is very easy and comes up many more times than you would suspect.

Simply shoot the cue ball into the rail *as close as possible to the object ball, without hitting it.* Use left English.

The cue ball comes off the rail into the object ball, and the kiss takes place off the gray ball. There is really no place for the object ball to go except down into the pocket.

To practice this, put the object ball one inch off the rail.

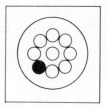

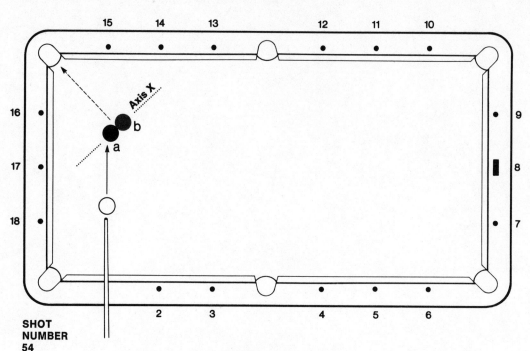

SHOT
NUMBER
54

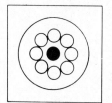

THE FROZEN KISS SHOT
No. 1

When a line drawn from the center of the pocket runs between two balls (or two balls not more than ⅛ inch apart), these balls are said to be "on".

Strike the cue ball as indicated. Use a center stroke, and make sure that you hit ball "A" enough to the right of axis "X" so that ball "A", as it kisses off ball "B", will go into the pocket.

Once you know the contact point, *try moving the cue ball around, and hitting the contact point at different angles.*

You will discover that you have wide latitude in this highly repetitive shot.

As we often have said, you must be able to see inside a cluster of balls, and pick out the anatomy of a familiar shot. Consider this version opposite :

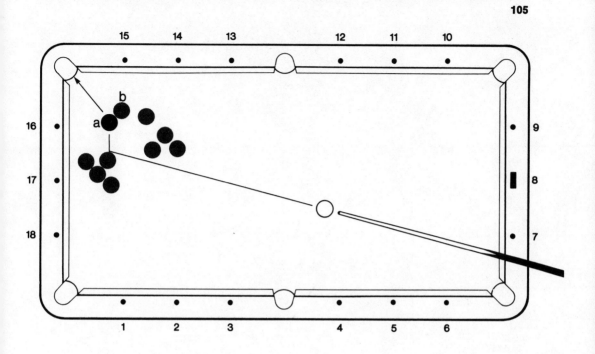

When you peer inside a cluster, you must look for the indirect as well as the direct shots!

You will see easy combinations where you thought none existed before.

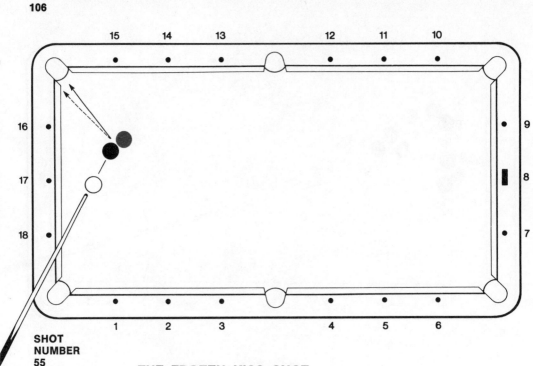

SHOT
NUMBER
55

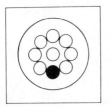

THE FROZEN KISS SHOT
No. 2

Here the two balls are not dead on the pocket, as in Shot No. 54 —so it looks like we have no shot.

Not so!

We shoot the cue ball at 6:00 o'clock, putting on strong draw. And—the object ball goes into the pocket!

These frozen kiss shots come up many thousands of times, and since a high percentage are not dead-on, this is an important part of your repertoire.

This shot will not work at any great distance, but when a fraction of the cushion stands between you and sinking the proper ball, it's a life saver!

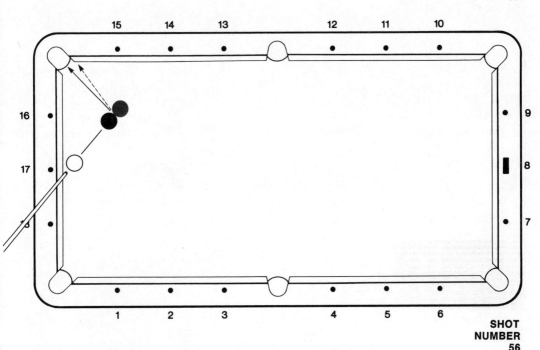

THE FROZEN KISS SHOT
No. 3

Here again the two frozen balls are not dead on. What's more, this time they are on the far side of the pocket.

Use the cue ball to pull the object ball back? "Impossible!" the average player would say. And—he would be wrong!

We stroke the cue ball at 12:00 o'clock, putting on follow. At the same time, we are careful to hit that object ball ¼ of an inch from the center, on the right.

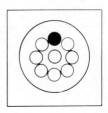

The ball rolls in!

Once again, the shot works for only a tiny fraction of the cushion, but it too is a life saver. You must experiment with this shot. You must use just enough force since too much, or too little, will spoil the shot.

It is much easier to make this shot if the gray ball is backed up by a second ball. The object ball has more weight to play against, and comes back more easily.

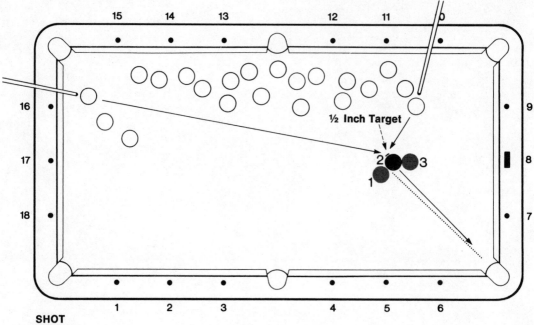

15   14   13   12   11

½ Inch Target

16   9

2 3
1

17   8

18   7

1   2   3   4   5   6

**SHOT
NUMBER
57**

THE DOUBLE KISS SHOT

Here, in slightly disguised form, is our old friend Shot No. 54. The two balls on the left (see dotted line) are just as much on, but that third ball (on the right) seems to fence us in.

But no! We have a lovely and shining shot, for we can now kiss off two balls!

What is more, as you can see from the diagram, we can shoot it from many more points on the table, for we have a much wider target area.

Simply hit the object ball on the target area. The object ball kisses off both gray balls and rolls into the pocket.

Shoot with medium speed.

As you can see, you can make the shot with the cue ball in an almost endless profusion of positions!

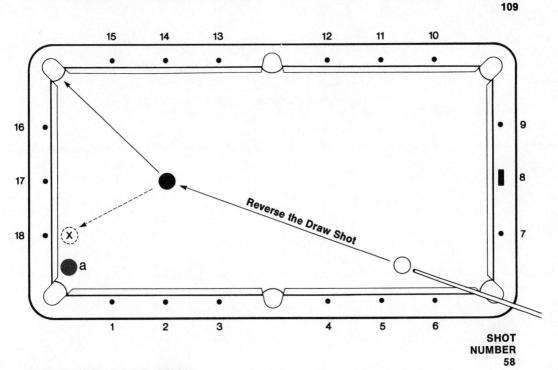

THE DRAW DRAG SHOT

This is one of the most critical shots in pool. We are not speaking of the exact placement of the balls above, but of the technique underlying this type of shot.

Here we must make a long shot down the table, but we wish to hit the object ball so slowly that the cue ball will roll only to "X", ready to sink ball "A". However, we face two big problems:

1. If we strike the cue ball slowly, it can roll off the direct line, and in a long shot we need *precision*.

2. If we strike the cue ball harder, we gain precision, but will never stop at "X".

The solution is to use "draw drag." Just as a Center Ball Shot will convert itself into forward roll (see Shot No. 3), so too will a long draw shot, *if hit at the proper speed.*

The "drag" from the fabric slows down the back spin, like this:

Draw shot hit at proper speed losing its backspin

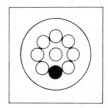

The result is that the cue ball hits the object ball softly, just as it is picking up forward roll.

Strike the cue ball with 6:00 o'clock draw. *Strike it just hard enough, so that by the time it hits the object ball it has only a bit of forward roll, with just enough strength to sink the object ball and coast to a stop at "X".*

You have enough speed for accuracy, but you hit the object ball gently!

Practice this until you know just the speed with which to draw. It is a vital shot in position play, and you will play it in thousands of variations.

Note: In the big diagram, the object ball is on the spot, and the cue ball behind the string. This itself is not an easy shot; but since you will shoot it many times, you might as well learn it.

However, if you wish to simplify practicing drag draw, put the object ball just outside the pocket, and arrange yourself a new "X", and a new ball "A".

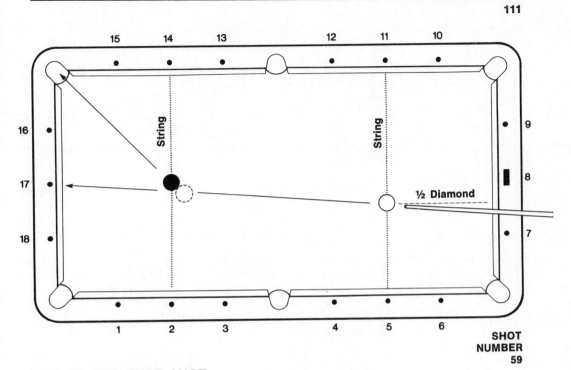

SHOT
NUMBER
59

THE ON THE SPOT SHOT

If ever there was an identical, constantly repeated shot in pool, here it is. In many types of games you will have the cue ball "in hand",* and be called on to sink a ball on the foot spot (see diagram page 173).

It's a long shot, and not easy, but it is very often *the* critical shot of a given game.

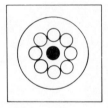

Here's a short cut that may make it simpler and easier. Put the cue ball on the head string, ½ diamond between diamond Nos. 7 and 8. The object ball is on the foot spot.

Ignore the object ball. Simply pretend it isn't there. Instead, shoot the cue ball to hit diamond No. 17. This brings the cue ball to the proper point of contact on the object ball, and roll it into the pocket.

---

* In Hand (See Glossary, page 213): The cue ball is *in hand* at the beginning of a game, i.e., you may place the cue ball wherever you wish behind the head string. Also, when your opponent scratches by sinking the cue ball in a pocket, you also then have the cue ball *in hand*.

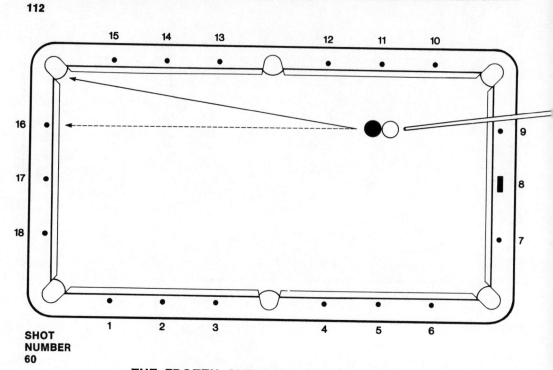

SHOT
NUMBER
60

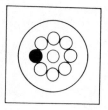

THE FROZEN CUE BALL SHOT
No. 1

Here the cue ball is frozen to the object ball, and both are lined up on diamond No. 7. It looks like an impossible shot, but it can be mastered in twelve or thirteen tries.

Raise the butt of your cue about 8 inches off the rail. Shoot softly, *coming in on the cue ball from slightly to the right of the ball* (notice the slant of the cue above), and strike at 9:00 o'clock. Complete your stroke with a smooth follow through. Don't just push the ball.

The object ball will roll down the black arrow.

Remember! It is a full stroke that does it—a soft stroke, with smooth follow-through.

Time after time you will find these two frozen balls on the table. It will pay you to set up different positions, and practice until you get the feel of this shot at different angles and positions.

This is, of course, a throw shot.

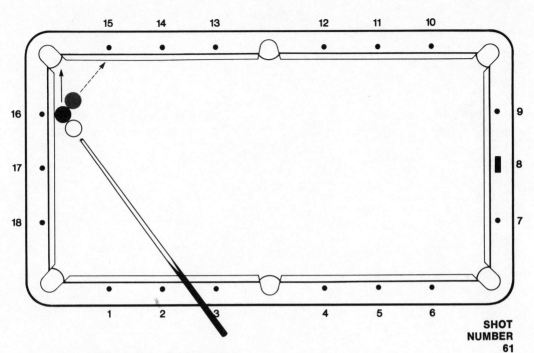

THE FROZEN CUE BALL SHOT
No. 2

Many times you run into the frozen cue ball shot where the cue ball is involved not with one, but with a cluster of two, three or even four balls. At first glance these seem to be trick shots. Not so! There are hidden mechanics underlying the interplay between the balls. *Once you understand these, in related situations you will find yourself producing miracle shots of your own.*

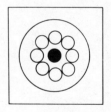

Consider the position above. The cue ball, and the gray ball, are ½ ball out from the cushion.

Shoot the cue ball softly in the center, straight ahead. The gray ball, in being pushed out of the way, acts really as a carom ball for the object ball. (Go back and look at Shot No. 50, to which this is first cousin.) The gray ball forms, for the moment, a channel, which directs the object ball into the pocket.

Don't ever expect to see this specific shot on a pool table—but expect, a thousand times, to run into the principle involved!

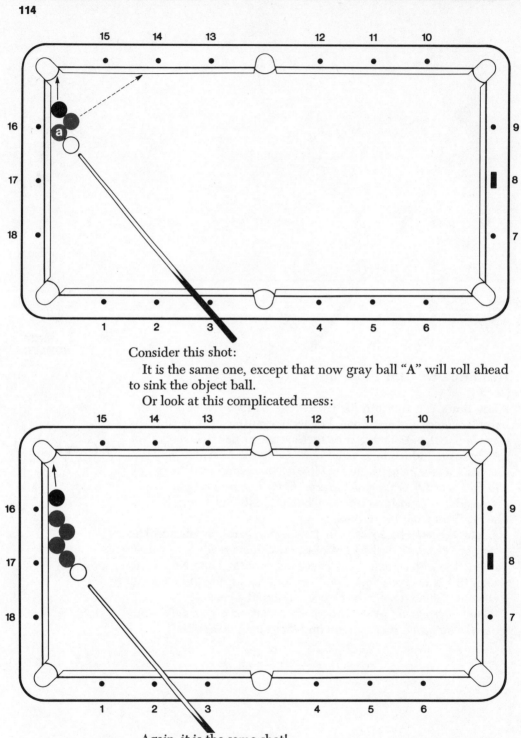

Consider this shot:

It is the same one, except that now gray ball "A" will roll ahead to sink the object ball.

Or look at this complicated mess:

Again, it is the same shot!

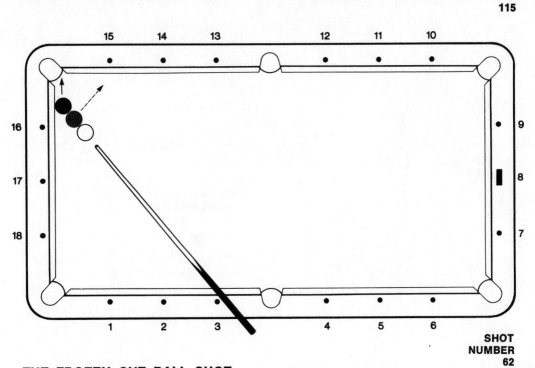

SHOT
NUMBER
62

THE FROZEN CUE BALL SHOT
No. 3

Once again, let us discuss a principle:

Here the three balls are in line, frozen to each other and the cushion. (Place the cue ball one ball's width from diamond No. 16.)

This time shoot the cue ball softly at 9:00 o'clock, and straight ahead. You will want the butt of your cue slightly to the right, and you will want to stroke, not push, the cue ball.*

As the gray ball is squeezed out, so to speak, it pushes the object ball into the pocket.

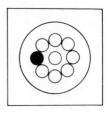

* A push stroke is legal if it is made with one continuous *stroke* of the cue, i.e., a *stroke* as opposed to putting the cue tip against the ball and pushing.

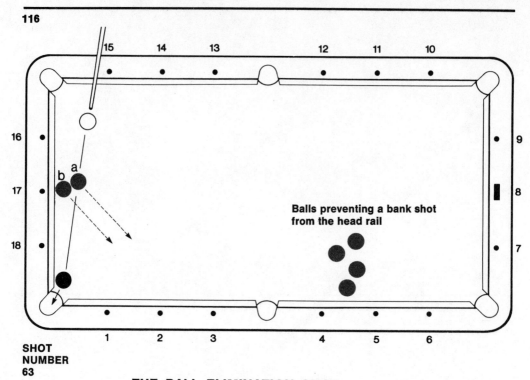

SHOT
NUMBER
63

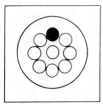

THE BALL ELIMINATION SHOT
No. 1

Here again is what may seem like a trick shot, and we introduce it in this book only to ask you to *concentrate on the interplay between the various balls.*

The player wishes to sink the black object ball. Unfortunately, because of other balls on the table, there is no way that he can hit it (by banking the cue ball from the head of the table, for example). After studying the position, he shoots directly at gray ball "A" using 12:00 follow. Both "A" and "B" vanish out of the way, the cue ball rolls down to the object ball and drops it into the pocket!*

Magic?

No. It is understanding of the interplay.

---

* Ray Martin once played this shot in a major tournament.

To understand the mechanics of this very beautiful shot, remove ball "B" and the object ball. You will then be left with this
position.

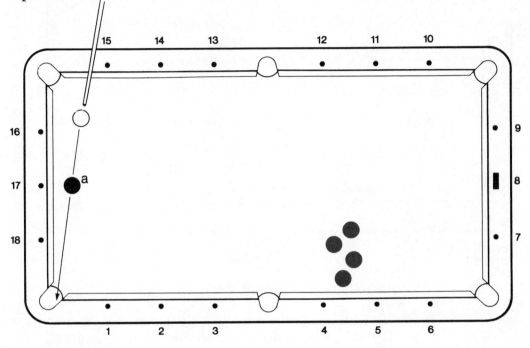

Now shoot ball "A" into the pocket (after all, they are directly
in line), using 12:00 o'clock follow on the cue ball, *so that the
cue ball follows it into the pocket.* Now you understand the
mechanics of the shot. Replace the object ball and ball "B", and
do the same thing again.

Ray Martin, in calculating this shot, realized that balls "A" and
"B" were so in line that a hit on one would whisk them both out
of the way.

It would take a 100-volume encyclopedia to catalogue the
interplay of balls, but once you know draw, follow and left and
right English, running and reverse English, you can begin to
work them out for yourself.

It is why, in a great tournament, you will watch a player study
a difficult shot for minutes, and then announce an unexpected
ball. He shoots and sinks it. And the crowd roars!

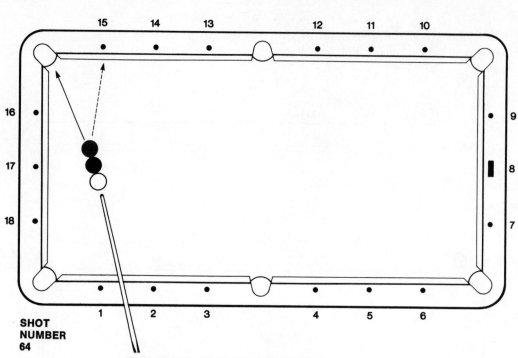

SHOT
NUMBER
64

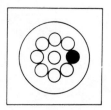

THE BALL ELIMINATION SHOT
No. 2

Here again is another shot based on the understanding of the interplay between balls. It is really nothing but a continuation of Shot No. 60 in a different position, with another ball frozen to the object ball.

Can we sink the black ball?

Yes! Hit the cue ball softly at 3:00 o'clock, shooting straight ahead. The gray ball will vanish to the left (because of the interplay, it *must*), and the object ball will drop into the pocket.

Let us give one more unobvious example (the truly beautiful shots in pool are always unobvious).

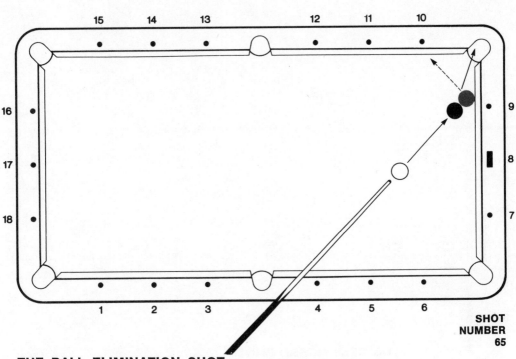

SHOT
NUMBER
65

THE BALL ELIMINATION SHOT
No. 3

The three balls happen to be in line, and the player must sink the black object ball. It seems blocked, and solidly blocked, by the gray ball.

Once again, we summon up the interplay between the balls!

We strike the cue ball hard, using the hardest possible draw.

The gray ball vanishes away, as indicated by the dotted line, and the black object ball spins into the corner pocket.

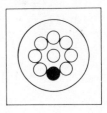

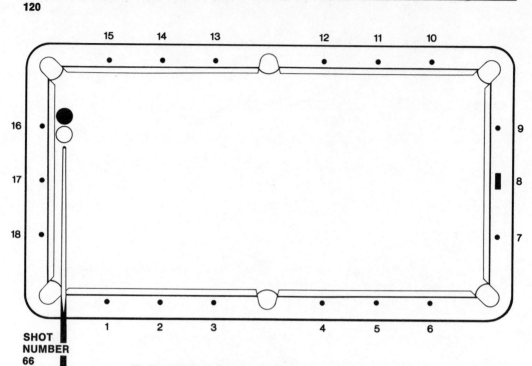

SHOT
NUMBER
66

THE SEMI-MASSÉ SHOT

Shot Nos. 6 and 8 were both Nip Shots. The balls were so close together that if you tried to follow through on your stroke, you would foul (the cue ball would rebound into your cue, giving you a double kiss).

What do you do when the two balls are too close even for a Nip Shot?

The answer is—the Semi-Massé.

Here the balls are ¼ to ⅛ inch apart. Elevate the butt of your cue until you have the angle shown below. Strike down in the center, as indicated, but follow through until the tip almost touches the cloth.

The ball will jump the tiny distance, kick the object ball into the pocket—while the cue ball remains almost stationary.

Many players, when they elevate the butt of the cue this much, prefer to hold the butt with their thumb toward them, and three fingers on the far side of the cue, rather than the usual grip.

Note: Full Massé shots are the most dazzling and beautiful of any shots executed with a cue stick. To the neophyte they are incomprehensible. However, the need for them does not arise in pool. Ray Martin, in his entire brilliant career, has never used a Full Massé Shot.

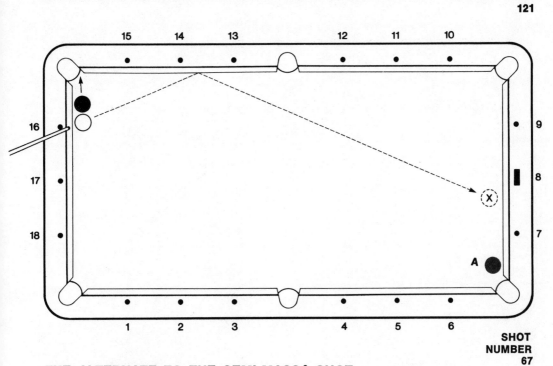

SHOT
NUMBER
67

THE ALTERNATE TO THE SEMI-MASSÉ SHOT—
TO PLAY POSITION

Here again, the balls are too close together even for a Nip Shot.
However, the Semi-Massé would leave the cue ball almost sta-
tionery, and we want to go down the table to get position on
ball "A".

Here we cut the object ball so that it will roll into the pocket,
and our cue ball angles off along the dotted line to "X".

This far along in our book, you need not be reminded that you
can strike center ball, or 9:00 o'clock, or 3:00, depending upon
where point "X" happens to be.

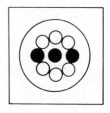

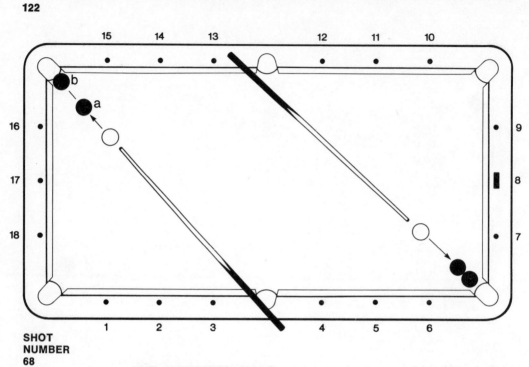

SHOT
NUMBER
68

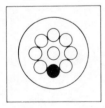

THE BONANZA SHOT

Here the balls are about 6 to 8 inches apart, and you propose to sink both balls with one shot! It's simple, it's easy and—it's not known to 9 out of 10 players!

Most players would shoot ball "A" into ball "B", a simple combination shot. However, there are two things wrong with such strategy: (1) Ball "A" may get out of hand, killing a chance for a second shot; (2) You sink only one ball.

Simply hit the cue ball with a strong draw. The backspin on the cue ball puts forward spin in ball "A". It rolls forward to sink ball "B", and then follows it into the pocket.*

The balls, naturally, must be in line, and you must hit ball "A" exactly in the center.

As you see from the diagram, you can make the same shot when the two balls are frozen and dead on the pocket.

* You can make the same shot with a hard center ball, but it is more difficult.

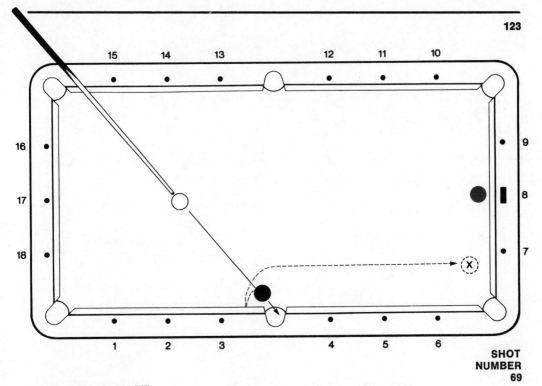

SHOT
NUMBER
69

THE HOOK SHOT

We have seen this shot used twice in the same game. Yet again, it is unknown to 9 out of 10 players, despite its great power in position play.

Put the cue ball on the spot. The object ball is ½ inch off the point of the side pocket, and ¼ of it overhangs the pocket. It's simple to sink the black ball, but how do you get your cue ball down the table for position?

Belt the cue ball at exactly 12:00 o'clock, *with only one object in mind, which is to sink the black ball.* The cue ball deflects to the right of its line of flight, but, since it has angular momentum, "hooks out" and runs down the table to "X".

Watch your opponent blink!

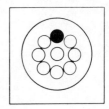

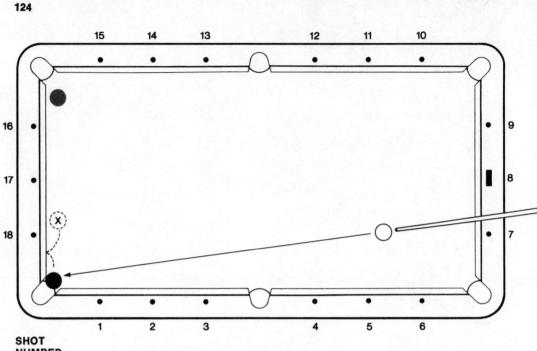

THE POCKET FACING SHOT

Time and again you will find the object ball stopped inside the jaws of the pocket, resting against the pocket facing. How do we shoot it in, but *stay down at that end of the table for position?*

The solution is a very easy shot, but far from obvious.

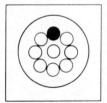

Stroke the cue ball at 12:00 o'clock, with medium speed. Hit the object ball inside the pocket ¾ full—whap! The cue ball will slam into the object ball, killing most of its energy with the ¾ impact. The forward motion of the ball, after a small rebound, will drive it slightly forward again.

The cue ball comes to rest at "X"!

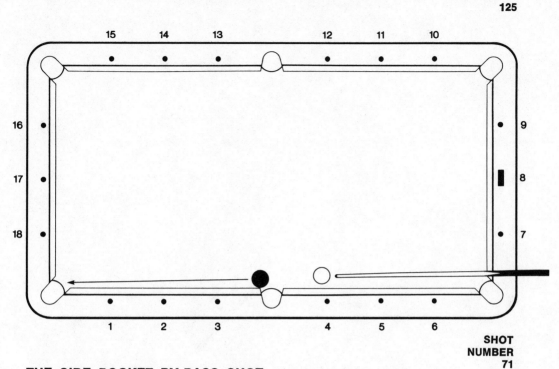

SHOT
NUMBER
71

THE SIDE POCKET BY-PASS SHOT

Here is a "trouble ball," literally overhanging the side pocket.
Our cue ball is slightly off the rail, about one inch, and we are
shooting inward.

Nine out of ten players would expect the cue ball to go into
the side pocket, and scratch.

It need not be!

Stroke the cue ball at 12:00 o'clock, or *perhaps a trifle lower.
But do add follow.* The cue ball will roll past the side pocket,
without scratching.

This shot has to be seen to be believed. In a recent tournament
a spectator offered 10 to 1 that the shooter would scratch. The
spectator lost.

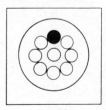

126

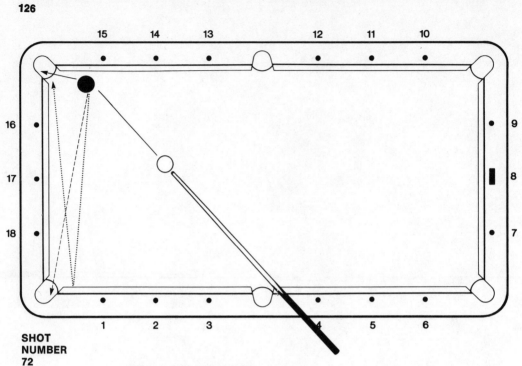

SHOT
NUMBER
72

THE POISON SHOT

Many a player has bitten the dust on this innocent-looking cut
shot. Shot at this angle, it is truly a poison shot, for you run into
trouble in two ways (the lines above show only the path of your
cue ball):

(1) You either scratch in the opposite pocket, or (2) You hit
the opposite cushion and return to scratch in the same pocket
in which you sank the ball!

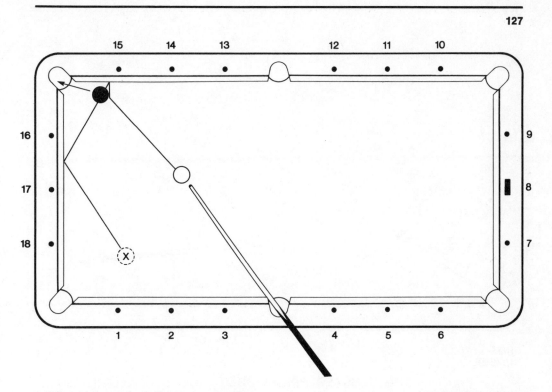

Here is a wonderfully easy solution:

Stroke the cue ball at 7:30 o'clock, and cut the object ball in. Use a soft stroke.

Your cue ball will follow the safe path shown by the solid line.

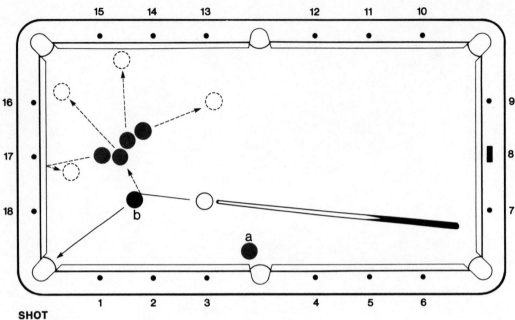

SHOT
NUMBER
73

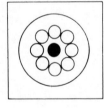

THE CLUSTER BREAK SHOT

When you watch an expert moving around the table, sinking ball after ball, the beginner is apt to overlook one of his important techniques—the cluster break.

For when three or four balls, or more, are huddled in a cluster, *the expert knows that these clusters represent bad future shots.* If he doesn't break them—perhaps no shots!

Here the beginner would sink ball "A". It is a cripple—an easy and certain shot.

Not the expert! He would cut in ball "B", carom off into that dense cluster and break them up. He knows he can always sink ball "A", but now he has arranged four other possible shots.

In addition (as you will see in our next shot) he also looks for "trouble balls," for even one ball can put a crimp in a high run!

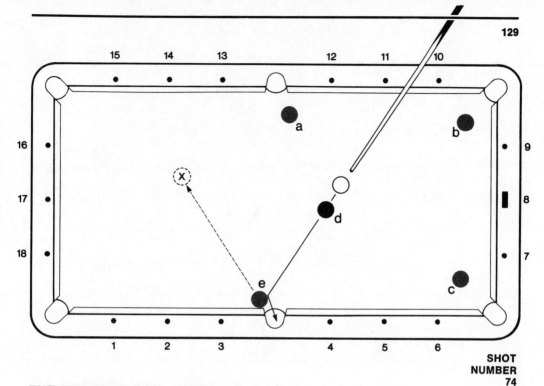

THE TROUBLE BALL SHOT

Even one ball, at some point, can shatter a high run. Ask yourself: "Is a ball inaccessible? Is it frozen to the cushion in an
awkward spot? Is it a possible scratch ball?"

Here is a good example:

The shooter has three easy balls, "A", "B", and "C". Instead, he
picks "D". He knows that if he ever has to use his cue ball against
"E", the cue ball would carom into the pocket, and scratch.

So, he shoots "D" into "E", an easy shot—and moves the trouble
ball out to "X".

*Pure position play, which is moving the cue ball into a good
position for a shot, is only part of the problem. You must visualize
the following shot, or shots, before you move the cue ball!*

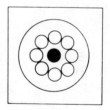

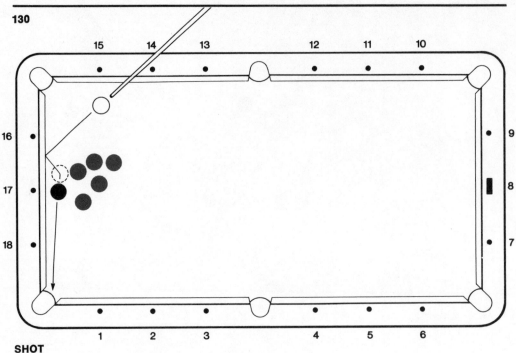

15   14   13   12   11   10

16   9

17   8

18   7

1   2   3   4   5   6

**SHOT
NUMBER
75**

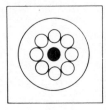

THE BY-PASS SHOT

Many times you will find no direct shot at all on the table, as in the position above. So we ask ourselves a triple question: "Are there any combination shots? Carom Shots? Or, Cushion Carom Shots?"

Here there are neither of the first two, but there is a dramatic (and frequent) carom interplay off the cushion that lets us by-pass all those trouble balls, and speed the object ball into the pocket.

Set up the balls as indicated, with the carom ball 1¼ inches from the cushion and the object ball ½ inch from the cushion. Shoot the shot as shown.

You will never see this shot *exactly*, but after you shoot it a few times, you will begin to get the feel of it, and store it away in that "eye, arm, and brain computer."

It will bail you out of many a tough spot!

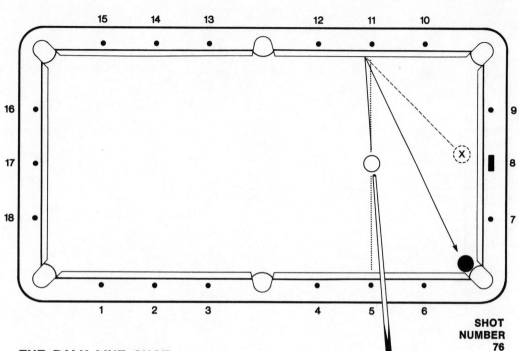

SHOT
NUMBER
76

THE BALK LINE SHOT

In pool games (Eight Ball, Nine Ball, Rotation) your opponent may scratch, i.e., his cue ball will go into a pocket. You then have the cue ball in hand, which means that you can place it anywhere you want behind the balk line.* However, *you must shoot forward of the balk line*.

What happens, then, when the ball you must next hit is behind the balk line?

Since a bank off the head rail is a difficult shot, try this:

Put the cue ball on the spot. Shoot the ball just ahead of the balk line, with 3:00 o'clock English. *Shoot very softly, so that you will get maximum* English. The cue ball will come back as shown, and sink your object ball.

You will face this situation hundreds of times. Experiment! You will find that you can bring the ball back as far as the dotted line. It is a most valuable, and often repeated, shot.

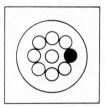

* In pool, head string and balk line are one and the same.

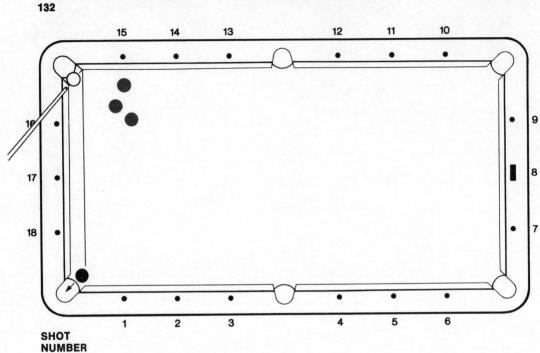

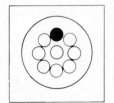

THE POCKET POINT SHOT

Your cue ball is trapped on the lip of the pocket, and frozen up against the pocket facing. You can't shoot down the table, because of certain obstruction balls. However, there's a shot waiting to be sunk across the table at the other pocket.

A hopeless situation? No, there's an out—a shot which looks zany, but isn't.

Shoot at the point of the cushion on the other side of the pocket. It's a bank shot, off the point, and your cue ball can go straight to the other ball!

This shot looks "hair-trigger" and difficult. It isn't. It's quite easy, and can keep you from breaking a high run.

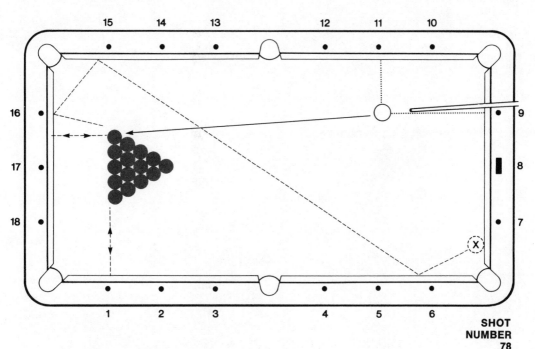

SHOT
NUMBER
78

THE OPENING BREAK SHOT

In straight pool (or 14.1) the man who has to break the rack is at a disadvantage. He must call each shot, and here the chance of sinking a called ball is microscopic. What is more, *if he breaks the rack, he may leave his opponent a shot and see him go soaring off on a high run.*

And worse! He must drive two of the balls to the cushion, plus the cue ball, or he fouls!

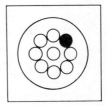

Here is the way the champions play it: Put the cue ball in the corner of the rectangle made by diamond Nos. 11 and 9. Aim to hit ½ of that corner ball. However, shoot at 1:30 o'clock, which will swerve the cue ball to the right so that you hit only ¼ of the ball.

Here's what happens: Your object ball will roll to the cushion and back almost in place. The impact through the line of balls sends the opposite corner ball to the cushion, and back almost in place. The cue ball, helped by that right English, goes off of three cushions, as shown, and comes to rest (you hope) frozen against the head rail.

Your opponent is left with an impossible shot.

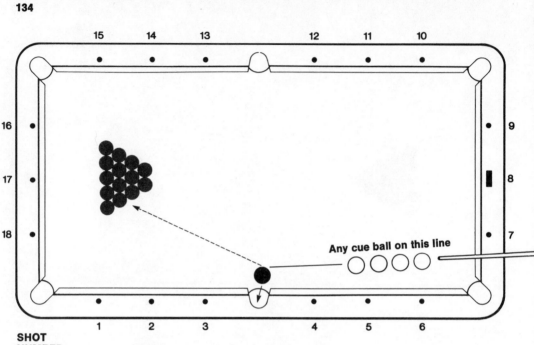

SHOT
NUMBER
79

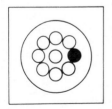

THE SIDE-POCKET BREAK SHOT
No. 1

Here we have the continuation of a 14.1 game. You have sunk the 14th ball. The 15th ball, your "break ball," is lying by the side pocket. The 14 balls have been re-racked, and *you wish to break again while you sink the 15th ball,* so that you can continue your high run.

In this position we have a powerful break shot.

Stroke the ball with strong draw at 6:00 o'clock. The object ball here is about ¼ inch off the point of the side pocket, so it is easy to sink, and the cue ball smashes into the rack with great force, scattering the balls, so that you can continue your run.

Why 6:00 o'clock? Try shooting the same shot with center ball. In a large number of cases, the cue ball will deflect off the side of the rack—and scratch.

Since you will rarely encounter this shot exactly, let's take a look at some of the principles:

Next your break ball is in the center of the side pocket, and the cue ball at a different angle. We shoot now at 3:00 o'clock, to get running English, hitting about ¼ of the object ball. The cue ball comes off the back rail to hit those two end balls—which is ideal. (If the cue ball were to hit in the center of the bottom of the triangle, the cue ball may not wind up in as good a position for the next shot.*)

* From the two end balls, the cue ball spins out and away. As we explain in more detail in Shot No. 85, there is less chance of the cue ball winding up in an unfortunate position in a cluster of freshly-broken balls. *This applies only to shots below the rack.*

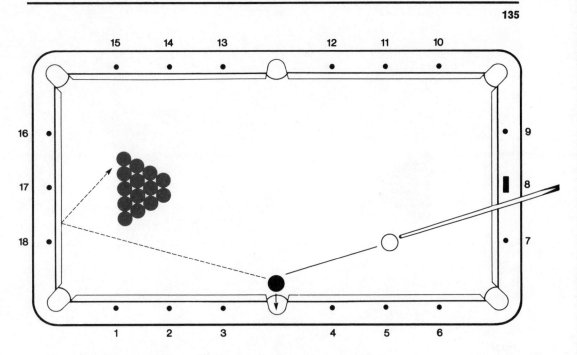

Consider the same shot with the cue ball on the spot. Here we stroke with 1:30 o'clock running English, and come off two cushions to strike those favored last two balls:

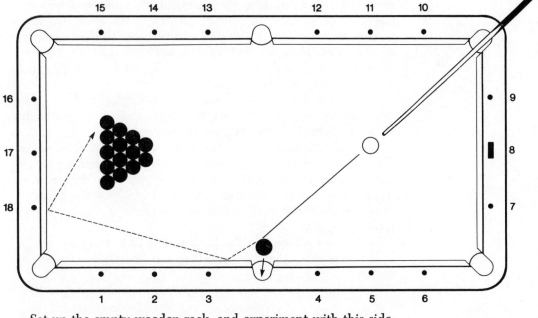

Set up the empty wooden rack, and experiment with this side-pocket shot from different angles. Where do you hit the pack?

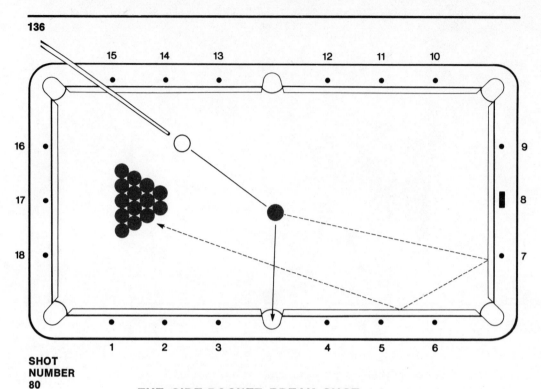

SHOT
NUMBER
80

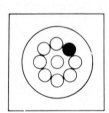

THE SIDE-POCKET BREAK SHOT
No. 2

Here the object ball is in the center of the table, and with the cue ball at yet another angle. Already, with what we have learned from Shot No. 79—*and by applying what we have learned in this book about coming off the cushions with English*—we know this: It is a rare side-pocket shot that doesn't give us a chance to smash into the rack!

Here we shoot at 1:30 to get running English and open the angle off the cushion. We sink the object ball, using a medium stroke, and come off two cushions to scatter the rack.

Where English is involved, we always specify a medium stroke. Since a high percentage of break shots involve caroming off the cushion, it is important that you keep in mind the difference in the *angle of carom* with a medium shot, vs. the *angle of carom* in a hard shot. *The hard shot closes the angle of rebound,* as we show in the next shot.

It does not follow that the hard shot is bad. You may need a hard shot to reach that rack. Just keep the difference in the angles in mind!

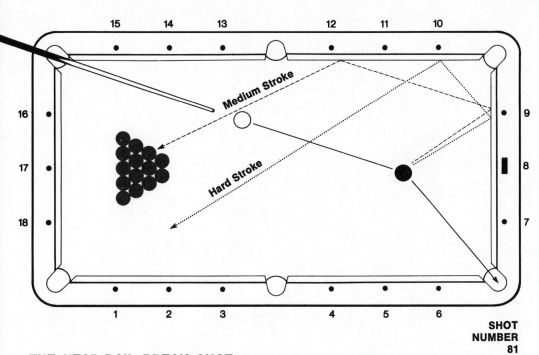

SHOT
NUMBER
81

THE HEAD-RAIL BREAK SHOT
No. 1

Reread the last two paragraphs in Shot No. 80. Then study closely the set of lines above.

Here the object ball is on the spot, and the cue ball in the corner of the rectangle drawn out from diamond Nos. 13 and 16.

Notice the difference between the dash lines and the dot lines.

If you shoot with a medium stroke, you smash into the pack. But if you shoot with a hard stroke you miss the pack entirely, for you have closed the angles of rebound—and here it is ruinous!

Let us repeat, a hard stroke is not always bad. There may be a break shot position where you'll miss the rack if you don't close those angles!

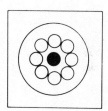

Note: The importance of speed on a cushion shot cannot be overemphasized. A soft stroke opens the angles, and a hard stroke closes the angles. It is why *control of speed* is one of the big secrets of pool.

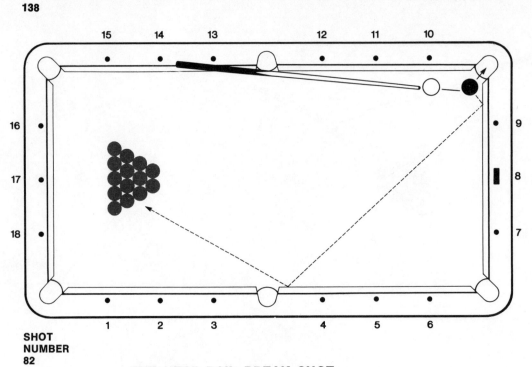

THE HEAD-RAIL BREAK SHOT
No. 2

Let us repeat again, we do not expect you to have one of these identical shots. But these are the *critical* shots (one might say "pattern shots"), and when you have fed all of these into that "eye, arm and brain computer," you are going to have very definite ideas of how to hit that rack from the head-rail *in any position.*

Place the two balls as shown. Shooting with medium speed again, hit the object ball *exactly in the center, so that it goes into the center of the pocket,* i.e., "splits the pocket." This means you hit about ⅛ of the object ball. Stroke the cue ball at 3:00 o'clock, to get running English.

Whack! Into the rack!

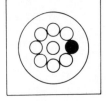

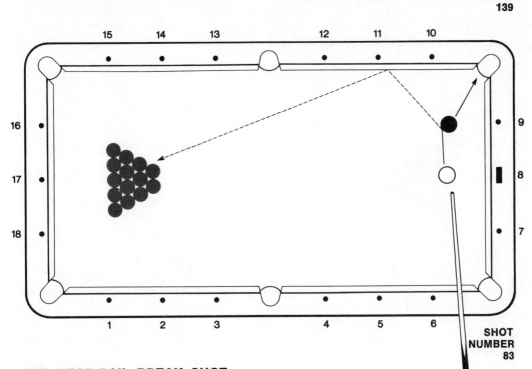

THE HEAD-RAIL BREAK SHOT
No. 3

Here is another essential critical shot where we are shooting in the opposite head pocket from Shot No. 82. This time we need come off only one rail to smash into the rack.

Stroke the ball at 7:30 o'clock to get running English. Cut the object ball to split the pocket using a medium stroke.*

As we said before, whack! Into the rack!

By now you should have a very clear idea of how to shoot a ball at any angle into a head pocket, and reach that precious rack!

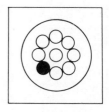

* Put the object ball ½ diamond off diamond No. 9. Put the cue ball the same distance from diamond No. 8.

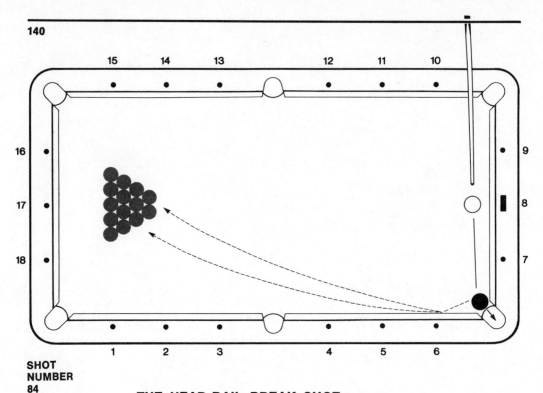

SHOT
NUMBER
84

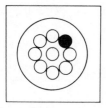

THE HEAD-RAIL BREAK SHOT
No. 4

Here is a shot not known to 9 out of 10 players, yet amazingly easy to execute.

Here the object ball is poised *almost* inside the corner pocket. Sinking it is one of the easiest shots in pool, yet—is there any way in the world to reach and break that rack?

The answer is "Yes!" And it is easy.

Stroke the cue ball at 1:30 o'clock. Hit exactly ½ of the object ball. It's spectacular the way the cue ball curves out, and spins down to hit the rack.

You must experiment three or four times with this shot to determine the right, firm stroke. The two arrows show what happens at two speeds. If you strike too hard, the curve of the ball will miss the triangle.

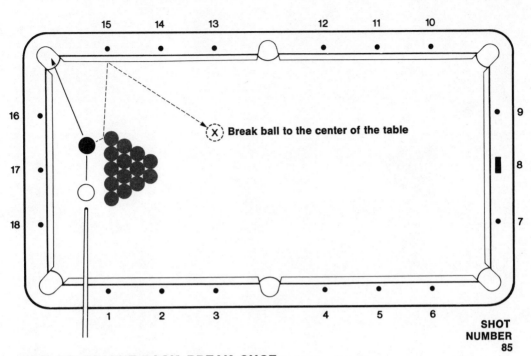

Break ball to the center of the table

SHOT
NUMBER
85

THE BELOW-THE-RACK BREAK SHOT
No. 1

Every straight pool player, in sinking his 14th ball (known as the
key ball), hopefully has selected a 15th ball as his *break ball* and
tries to maneuver his cue ball into a position for the ideal break.

Here we have *almost* the ideal shot from below the rack.
Notice that the cue ball and the object ball are the same distance
from the rail.

Stroke the cue ball with 1:30 English, and the cue ball should
smash into those two ideal end balls,* so that it not only breaks
the rack, but goes on to the cushion at diamond No. 15, where
the 1:30 English spins it out to the center of the table, giving you
a much better chance for future shots.

*Always, if it is possible, when breaking from below the rack,
go for those two end balls in such a way (or with such English)
that your cue ball heads for diamond No. 15 and goes up the
table. The odds are that you will get a better next shot.* Many
great high runs have been interrupted when the cue ball stops
in a hopeless position in a cluster of freshly broken balls.

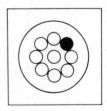

* Reread the footnote for Shot No. 79.

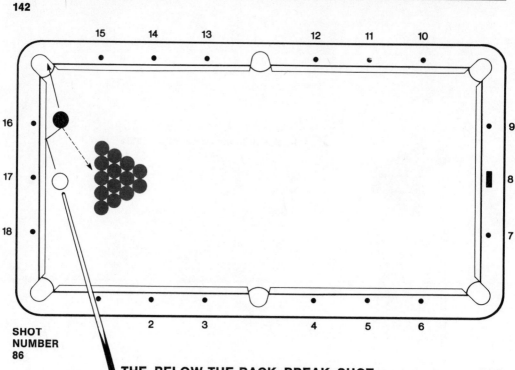

SHOT
NUMBER
86

THE BELOW-THE-RACK BREAK SHOT
No. 2

Put each ball 1 inch off diamond Nos. 16 and 17. Is there a way to get the cue ball back into the rack?

Turn back to our old friend, Shot No. 36. By now you should be expert at it, and this break shot is only a variant.

Stroke the cue ball at 6:00 o'clock, with your most perfect draw. *Use no English.* Hit the rail first, at the proper angle to sink the object ball. Use moderate speed.

In the U.S. Open in Chicago, one of the top players in the United States, not knowing this shot, played a safety!*

* If you don't know what "a safety" is in straight pool (or 14.1), see the Official Rules, p. 181.

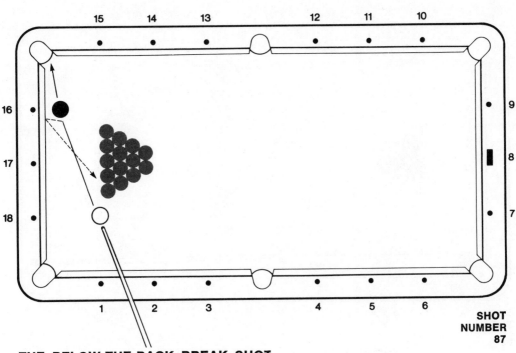

SHOT
NUMBER
87

THE BELOW-THE-RACK BREAK SHOT
No. 3

Study the lie of the two balls in the previous shot, and study the position here. The object ball is in the same place. The cue ball, however, has been moved out to the corner of a rectangle drawn out from diamond Nos. 1 and 18.

No need, now, to go to the rail *before* hitting the object ball. We go to the rail *after* hitting the object ball.

Again, we stroke with our most flawless draw. However this time we draw at 7:30 o'clock, adding a little left English to throw the ball into the cushion on the left. The cue ball not only spins back off the rail, but *hits the two end balls at the foot of the rack*. Reread the last paragraph in Shot No. 85 to see why this is ideal.

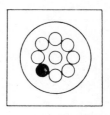

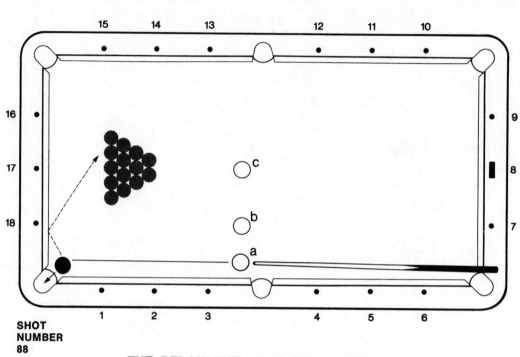

SHOT
NUMBER
88

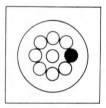

THE BELOW-THE-RACK BREAK SHOT
No. 4

In this shot you are going to learn three ways to sink that ball in the corner pocket, and come off the rail to hit those two ideal end balls.*

Place cue balls "A", "B" and "C" as indicated. (Note that "B" and "C" are in line with diamond Nos. 18 and 17.)

With cue ball "A", stroke at 3:00 o'clock, with medium speed, hitting ¼ of the object ball. The cue ball will travel as indicated, coming in directly on the two ideal end balls.

Now to cue ball "B". The angle here is much sharper, and we want to use draw to *go into the cushion.*

* Reread Shot No. 85.

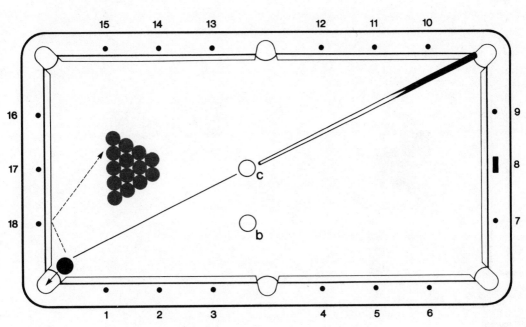

The draw here is at 4:30 o'clock, again to throw the cue ball into the cushion. This time we hit ½ the object ball.

The shot with cue ball "C" is exactly the same, except that this time we hit ¾ of the object ball.

Don't the principles begin to become crystal clear?

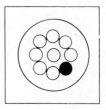

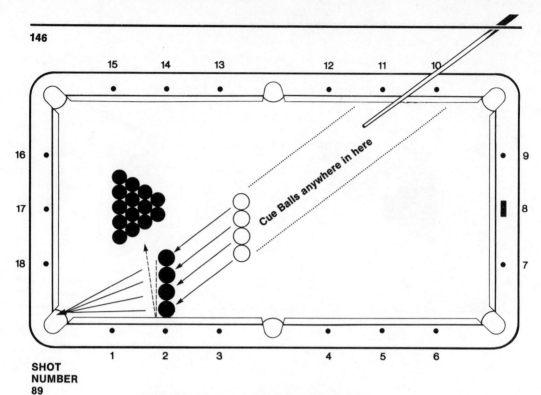

SHOT
NUMBER
89

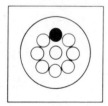

THE 12:00 O'CLOCK BREAK SHOT

Here we have four object balls and four cue balls to show the approximate space where a large number of cue and object balls might be.

Every object ball is a break ball.

Stroke the cue ball at 12:00 o'clock, sinking each object ball in the corner pocket. The cue ball (within limits) follows the principle of the broken arrow, i.e., it goes into the cushion, then spins back into the rack for a fine break.

We are not so much concerned here with exact placement as with the *principle*. Every shot you ever shoot will have to come out of that "eye, arm, and brain computer." So set up a rack. Experiment! Before long you will know the exact limits of the 12:00 o'clock Break Shot.

Note: It is obvious, in the above diagram, that if all four cue balls were shot at all four object balls *at the same angle*, we would not sink all object balls.

We assume that by this time you know how to sink balls. Consider the angles and the cue stick in the above diagram as roughly illustrative of a principle.

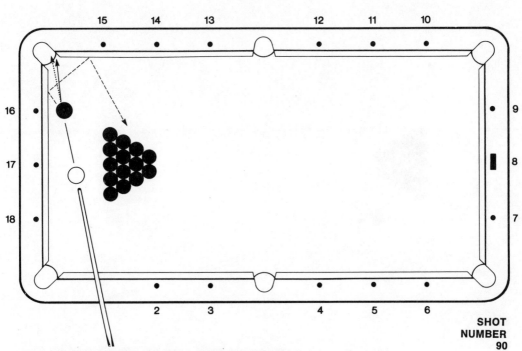

SHOT
NUMBER
90

THE CHEAT-THE-POCKET BREAK SHOT

Here the two balls are straight on the corner pocket, as we can
see from the dotted line. There seems to be no way to get that
cue ball to fight back to the rack.

But—yes! Go back to Shot Nos. 4 and 24 for a frequently use-
ful technique—cheating the pocket.

We stroke the cue ball at 12:00 o'clock, to get strong follow.
We hit the object ball slightly to the left, so that instead of
splitting the pocket we go to the pocket facing. The cue ball is
deflected into the cushion, spins to the next cushion, and rips
into the rack!

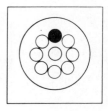

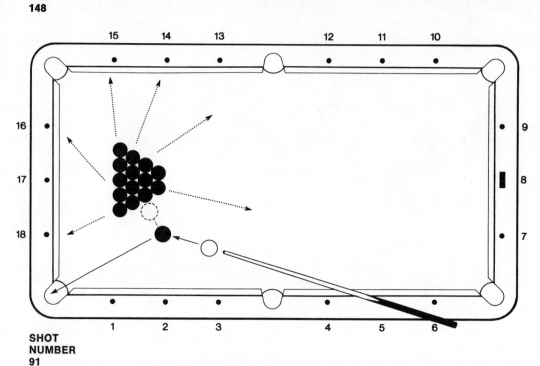

SHOT
NUMBER
91

THE IDEAL BREAK SHOT

Of all possible break shots, is one better than all the rest? The answer is "Yes!" It is the shot above, and it is one of *the* critical shots in pool.

It is easy to shoot. It can be shot with great force. The cue ball hits the rack with the power and position to scatter the balls widely.

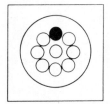

Stroke the cue ball at 12:00 o'clock, to get full follow on the ball. Shoot with a hard stroke. Wham! The pack is scattered to the winds!

Here is why this particular shot is so critical. After 13 balls have been sunk, you are left with two balls. The one you plan to sink next is known as your "key ball" *because it is the key to getting position on your last, or "break ball".* As you sink the key ball, you try to position the cue ball so that it will give you a fine break shot.

Among fine players, time after time after time it is almost the identical shot above! They have sunk their last 4, 5, 6 or 7 shots just to bring this about. They know it's the ideal break shot, the best one for continuing a high run.*

* Keep in mind that you can put this break shot on any one of the three sides of the triangle.

And keep in mind that "ideal" is a somewhat flexible concept. We can move the cue ball further away, or move both balls closer to the cushion. The question is: Is the shot clean enough to be almost certain and—will the carom of the cue ball smash those racked balls?

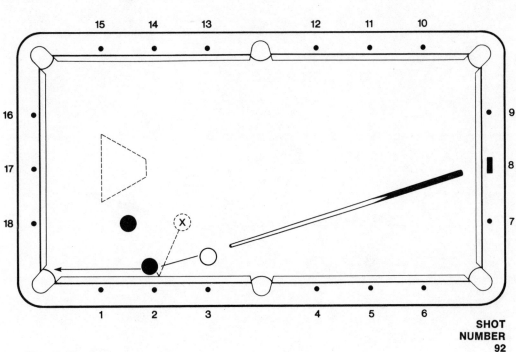

SHOT
NUMBER
92

THE KEY BALL SHOT
No. 1

Here the object ball is your key ball. As soon as you sink it, some-one is going to reach for the rack. So, you want to draw your cue ball back to "X", to get the *ideal break shot*.

Draw the cue ball at 6:00 o'clock. The result? If you shoot at just the right speed, you stop at "X".

Once again, keep in mind that this shot can be on any one of the three sides of the triangle.

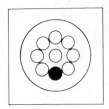

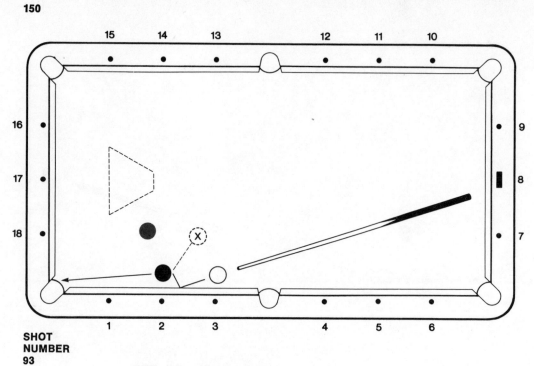

SHOT
NUMBER
93

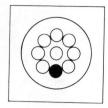

THE KEY BALL SHOT
No. 2

Here the two balls are equidistant from the rail. Each ball is ¼ inch from diamond Nos. 2 and 3.

Here we hit the rail first, using 6:00 o'clock draw. If you hit the cue ball properly enough to sink the object ball, and with just the right speed, the cue ball will roll back naturally to stop at "X".

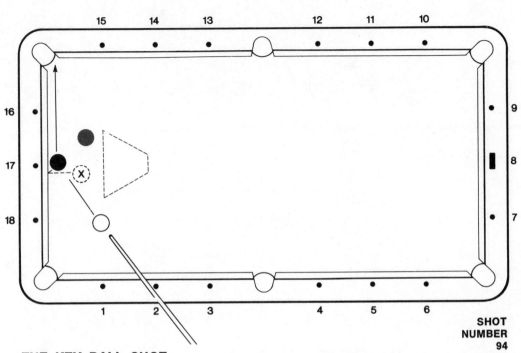

THE KEY BALL SHOT
No. 3

Unlike the two previous shots, here the object ball does not have to be pulled back in one way or another. All we have to do is sink the object ball, and bring the cue ball straight out from the cushion.

What witchcraft should be applied?

Simply shoot softly at 7:30 o'clock. Again we throw the ball into the cushion, but we are throwing it into the cushion with reverse English.* The English is against the cushion, against the roll of the ball. The result? the ball rolls gently out to "X".

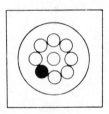

* See "Running English vs. Reverse English," page 55.

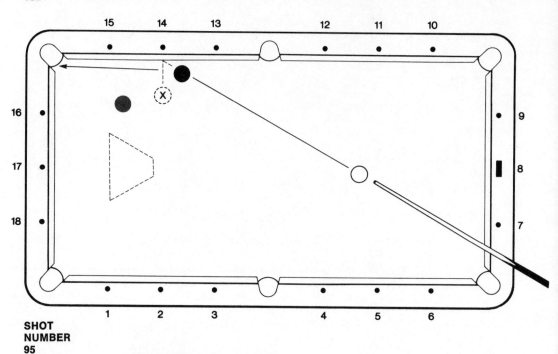

SHOT
NUMBER
95

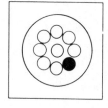

THE KEY BALL SHOT
No. 4

What's this? The same shot, on another side of the triangle? Of course it is! But if you shoot it in the same way, you will never make your *ideal break ball* position in a thousand years.

No two shots are ever really identical, and each shot must be appraised on its own, and checked for speed, angle and distance.

Right away we see that reverse English here is at 4:30, but that isn't all. *The ball is on the spot, a long distance down the table.* If we shot it gently enough to roll the cue ball out just to "X", the ball would have picked up forward roll. So we are right back to our old friend the Draw Drag Shot.* We stroke the ball for draw, putting on just enough back spin so that the cue ball, when it hits the object ball, can roll it into the pocket and come gently out to "X"!

* See Shot No. 58, the Draw Drag Shot.

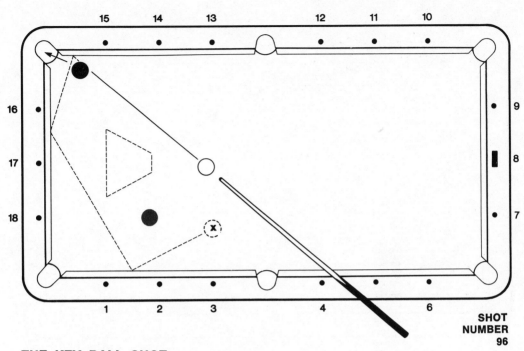

THE KEY BALL SHOT
No. 5

Since setting up the ideal Break Shot is of paramount importance in straight pool, you must summon up all that you know about English, angles, speed of stroke and cushion rebound to *see if you can get this ideal Break Shot from any point on the table.*

Here the break ball and the object ball are on the other side of the rack. Is all lost?

Indeed not!

When we study the situation for a moment, we resolve that if we can add running English, we should be able to carom off three cushions. So we shoot at medium speed at 10:30 o'clock. The result, when properly shot, is—perfection!

The wise player, of course, plots the progression in which he will sink his last 4, 5, 6 or even 7 and 8 balls, so that he can maneuver the ideal Break Shot. Then shot after shot in this book can be used to put the cue ball in spot "X". It may be a Follow Shot (Shot No. 5), a Draw Shot (Shot No. 7), a Throw Shot (Shot No. 16), one of the Running-Reverse Basic Position Shots (Shot No. 22), a Cheat-the-Pocket Side Shot (Shot No. 24), or a Side-Pocket Break Shot (Shot No. 80).

Turn back through these critical shots. Visualize your break ball on any side of a "ghost rack." See how they might play.

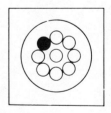

For example, do you recognize this?

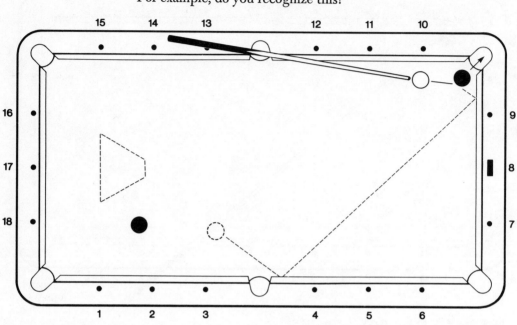

It's Shot No. 82, with 3:00 English, adapted to give us a fine break!*

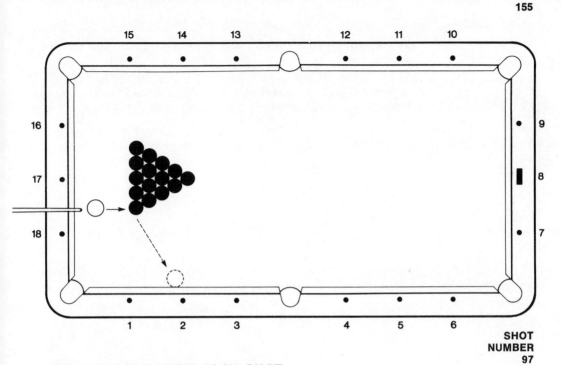

THE CLASSIC SAFETY PLAY SHOT
No. 1

No straight pool player lives who hasn't faced this shot a thousand times! The break ball has been restored to the rack,* it's your shot, and *you have no way to sink any ball.*

So, you must play a safety. The rule for a safety is:

". . . (The) player must drive an object ball to a cushion, pocket an object ball, or cause the cue ball to strike a cushion after contacting object ball."

Here the cue ball is at right angles to the rack, and is in line with the end ball. Shoot softly, at 10:30 o'clock, and shoot to hit exactly ¼ of the end ball, like this:

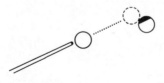

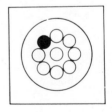

* This shot comes about when your opponent has no good break shot, calls a safety, and sinks the break ball. The break ball is then put in the rack, leaving you no shot.

The same thing happens when the break ball and cue ball stop inside the racking area. In this case all 15 balls are reracked.

You could obviously make this same shot from any of the three sides of the triangle.

The end ball should go to the cushion, and the cue ball should stay in the slightly loosened rack, *leaving your opponent no shot.*

What happens when the two balls aren't in line? Let's see.

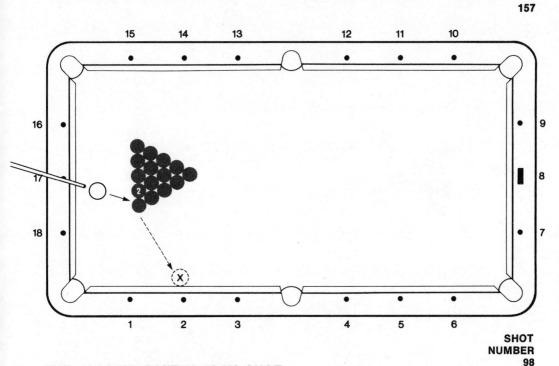

SHOT
NUMBER
98

THE CLASSIC SAFETY PLAY SHOT
No. 2

Here the cue ball is not in line with the end ball, but with the second ball on that side of the rack. However, despite the different angle, hit the end ball in exactly the same place, i.e., hit ¼ of the ball.

But this time shoot softly and use 6:00 o'clock draw. The cue ball will pull over just in front of ball No. 2, and again with a slightly loosened rack. The end ball should go to the same place, to "X", leaving your opponent no shot!

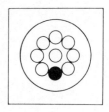

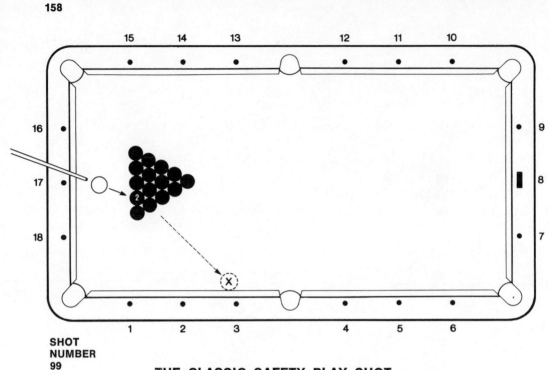

SHOT
NUMBER
99

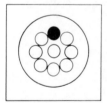

THE CLASSIC SAFETY PLAY SHOT
No. 3

Here the cue ball is in line with the center ball. Do we still have this classic safety play?

We do!

Shoot to a ball on either side of the center ball, using 12:00 o'clock follow, hitting this ball one hair toward the center ball. (In this case, since we are still shooting at ball No. 2, we would hit it one hair to the left.)

Notice! This time another ball moves out to "X". Again the cue ball stays in the loosened-up rack, leaving your opponent no shot.

And again, you can make such a shot from any side of the triangle!

SOME CLUSTER SHOTS- A TEST FOR YOUR EYE!

Time and again, in these 99 critical shots, we have said that you must be able to "see" the shot buried deep down inside a cluster of balls.

One of the great thrills of a tournament is to see a player baffled because he has no shot. He walks forward, leans over, and studies intensely the cluster and the lie of the balls. He turns his head this way, that way, squints, broods, crouches to look at different angles. Then he walks back to his cue ball, calls a shot, and shoots. The ball rolls in, and there is a storm of applause.

These look like witchcraft shots, superlative skill, miracle shots. Yet thousands of times *they are easy shots*, but so buried in the cluster that they are hard to see.

Here's a random selection, and every one of them is a shot that you now know. Study these clusters. Cover the solution printed below until you can *see* the shot concealed by the other balls.

159

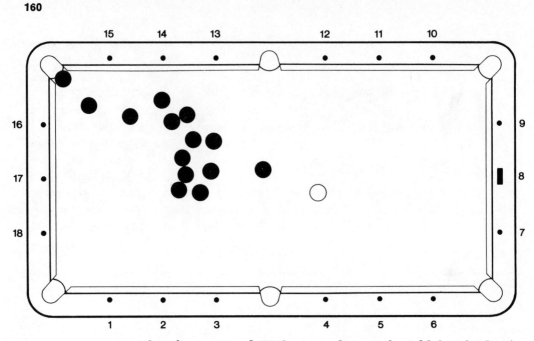

A hopeless position? With not a shot on the table? Indeed no! This is an easy shot, and what's more *it's a shot you now know!* Study the balls until you *see* it.

Solution: It's our old friend, the "By-Pass" Shot—Shot No. 75. Go back and restudy it, for you will be shooting it thousands of times. It's one of the most common shots in pool!

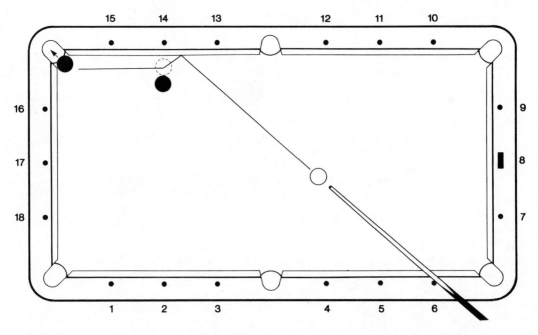

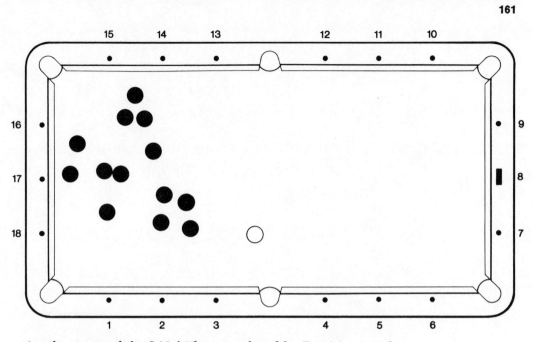

Another impossibility? No! This was played by Ray Martin in his second match for the World's Championship. His opponent later said: "Ray, I didn't *see* it."

Solution: It's another old friend, the first of our "Ghost Ball" Shots—the second diagram in Shot No. 48. It's hard to *see,* because three other balls are used to bring it off.

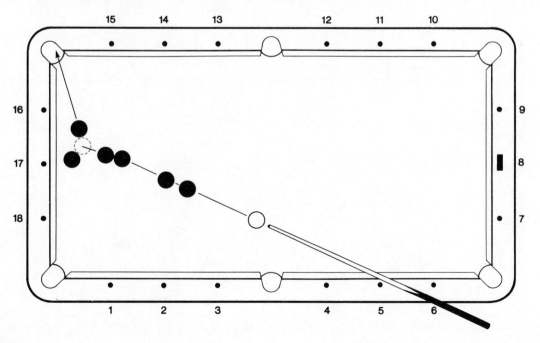

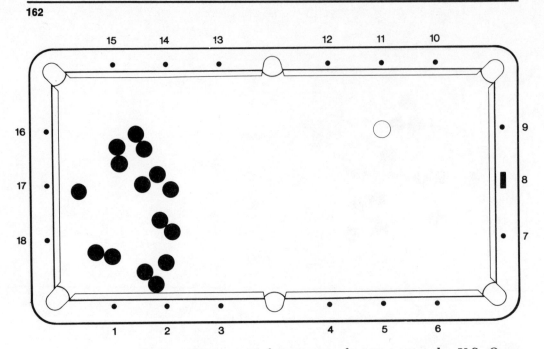

We set this one up for a man who once won the U.S. Open Championship. He studied the table for five minutes, and then bet $10.00 that there was no shot. He lost!

Solution: It's another of our seemingly miraculous "Ghost Ball" Shots— Shot No. 51. Again, go back and reread all of the details, for this one involves a little-known use of English.

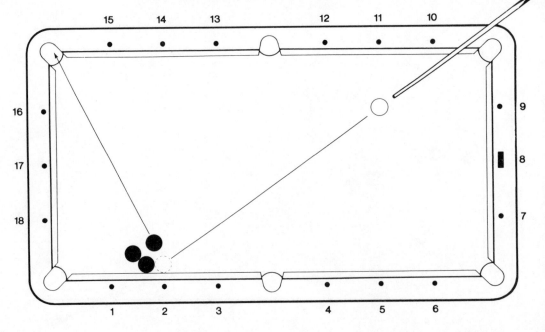

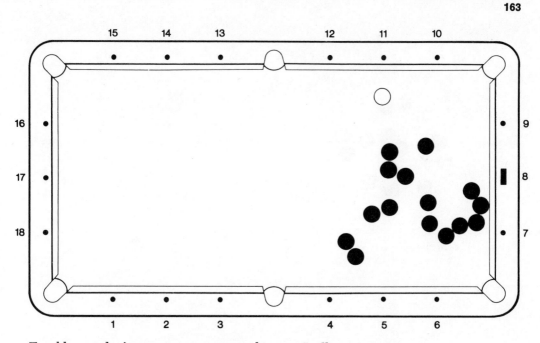

Frankly, we don't expect you to guess this one. It illustrates again the fact that other balls are often used to bring about a shot that you have practiced in simpler form.

Solution: It's the "Rail Kiss" Shot—Shot No. 53. Once again, three other balls are used to bring it off. *You must train yourself to look for sequences using other balls!*

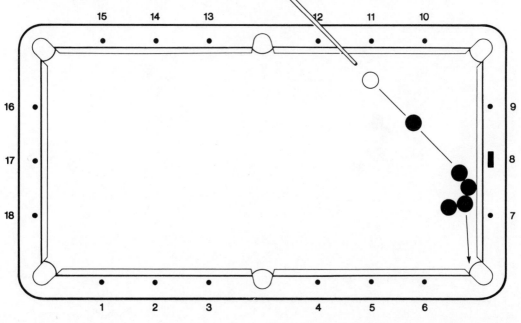

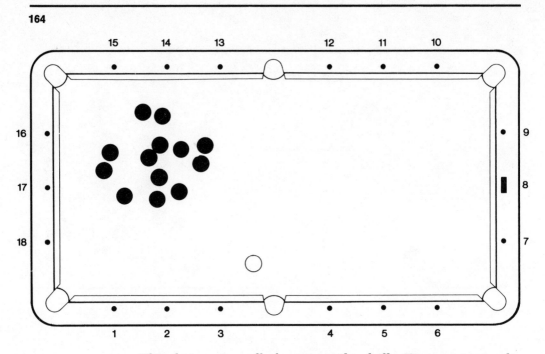

This shot, again, calls for using other balls. First, try to see the simple shot itself. Then, if you can't make it directly, see if you can bring it off *indirectly*.

Solution: It's one of the easiest of our entire book, the "Frozen Kiss" Shot —Shot No. 54. This shot is very often found in very dense clusters. It pays to study clusters!

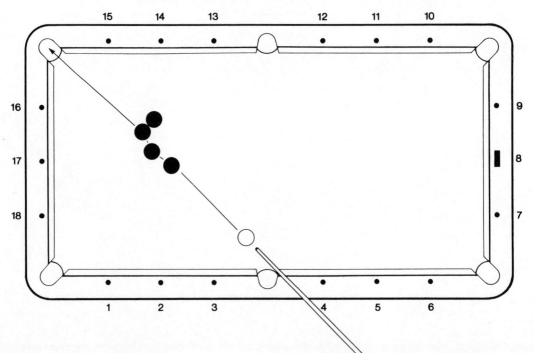

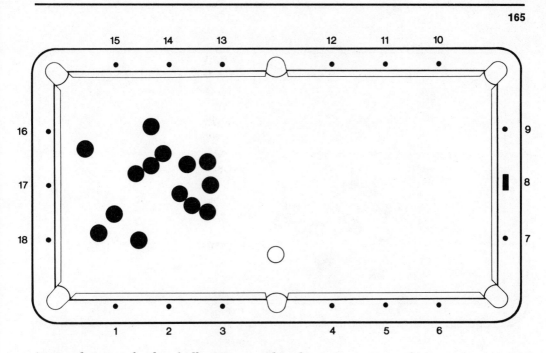

Again, the use of other balls. We saw this shot win a storm of applause in the U.S. Open Championship. And yet, it's so easy a child of ten can make it ten out of ten times!

Solution: It's the "Double Kiss" Shot—Shot No. 57. In disguised form, it's our old friend Shot No. 56, with a third ball that looks like it ruins the shot, but doesn't!

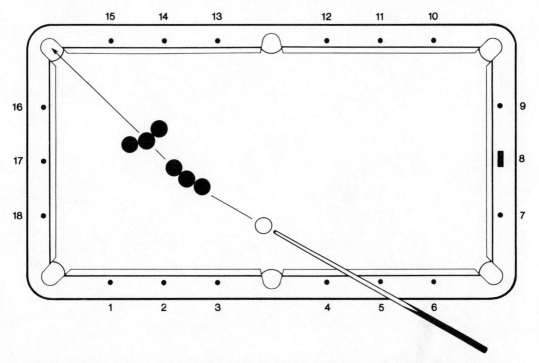

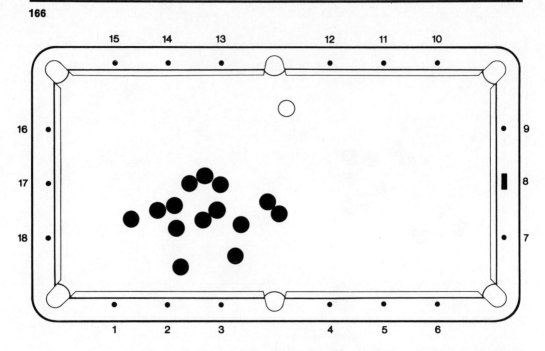

If you don't get this one, you're slipping! We predict again that a child can make it ten out of ten times. And yet, some of the best players in the world don't know it!

Solution: It's our "Ghost Ball" Shot again—the third diagram in Shot No. 48. It remains a fact that this terribly easy shot is difficult to *see.*

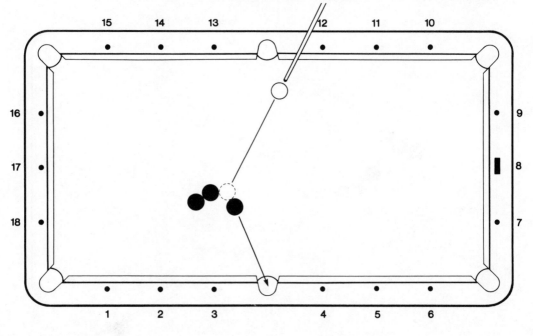

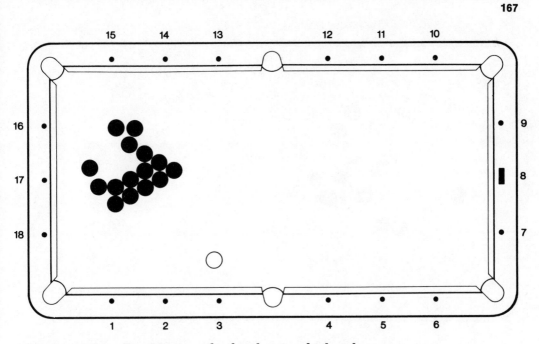

It was watching Ray Martin make this shot, in a high stakes game, that led to the writing of this book. "If you can't make *this one*," said Ray, "you can't make any!"

Solution: Once again, it's the "Frozen Kiss" Shot—Shot No. 54. Let us repeat, this shot is very often found in very dense clusters. The denser the cluster, the harder you look!

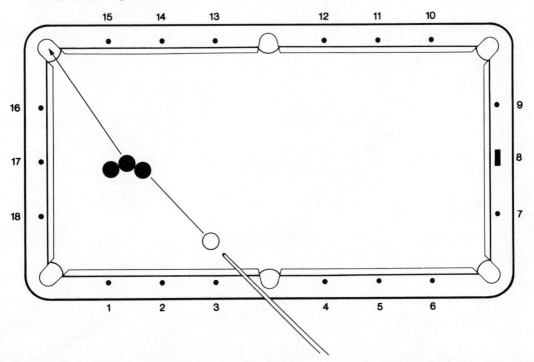

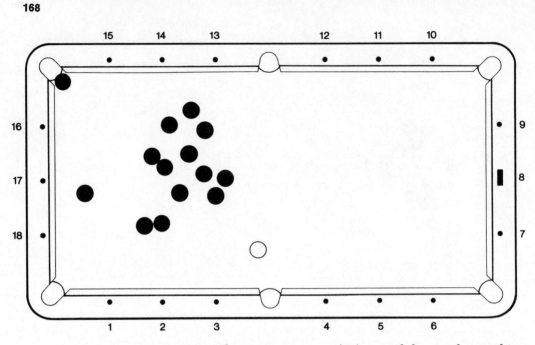

Here's one we *do* expect you to get! It's one of the simplest in this book, and yet one that comes up time and time again. It, too, lurks in dense clusters.

Solution: It's the "Dead On" Shot—Shots No. 12 and No. 13. It simply can't miss, when the balls are properly aligned, and here it is used to sink a ball near the pocket.

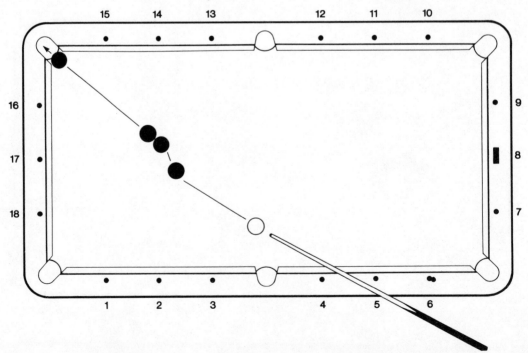

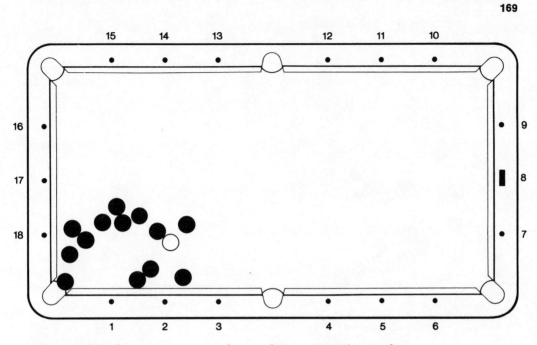

Again, a shot that many strong players do not *see*. It's not that they don't know the shot, it's just that they sometimes overlook it? So—study clusters!

Solution: It's the "Interference Ball" Shot—Shot No. 42. How many times this shot will save you when the cue ball is frozen against some other ball, and you're desperate!

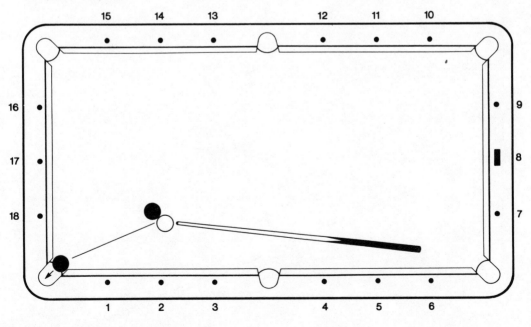

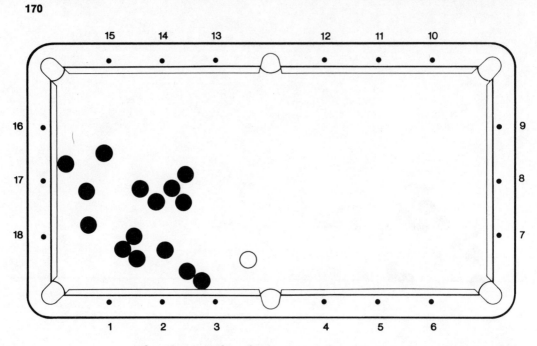

This shot is taken from one of Ray Martin's famous games. He sank his ball, and continued for a run of 115 balls to win the game. But again, you must *see* it!

Solution: It's our "Nudge Shot"—Shot No. 52. As we said earlier: "Once you have mastered it, it will become one of your secret weapons." Remember! *It pays to study clusters!*

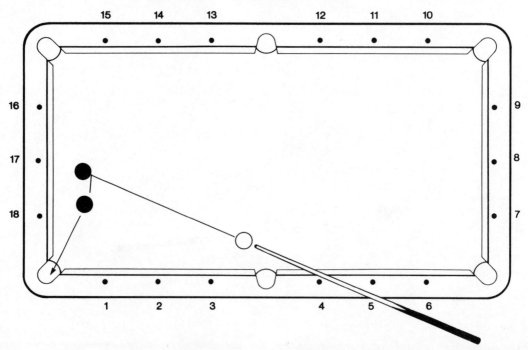

THE OFFICIAL RULES

Depending on the locality, there are many dozens of games which are played, and many of them with local rules.

However, over the years about 18 games have emerged which are the steady favorites of most of the pool players. The greatest of these (and "The Game of the Champions") is variously described at "Straight Pool" "14.1", "Continuous", or "14.1 Continuous", all of which means that you start with a rack of 15 balls, sink 14 balls, leave one ball on the table as your break ball—and then, if you are good, run from rack to rack into a high run.

Beyond this most ideal of all pool games, the others which are most popular are Eight Ball, Cowboy, Nine Ball, Bottle Pool and One Pocket.

The official rules of all of these games are published by the Billiard Congress of America, 717 North Michigan Avenue, Chicago, Illinois, 60611. This is a non-profit organization which has kindly permitted us to reproduce the rules of the most popular games for this book.

Their book, "The Official Rules and Record Book for All Pocket & Carom Billiard Games", belongs in the library of every pool player.

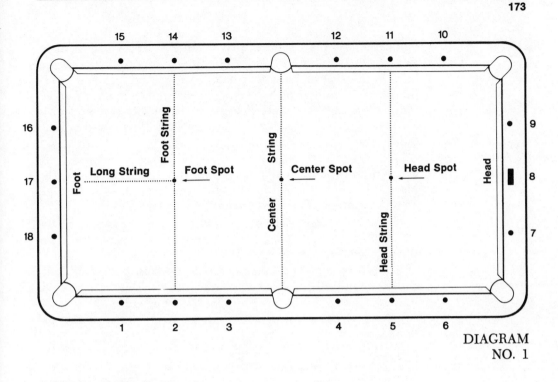

DIAGRAM
NO. 1

GENERAL RULES

All pocket billiard games are played on a rectangular table twice as long as it is wide. The table may be 3½-by-7 feet, 4-by-8 feet, 4½-by-9 feet, or 5-by-10 feet.

This game is played with fifteen object balls, numbered from 1 to 15, and a white cue ball. The cue ball is used to strike the object balls. The object balls are racked on the foot spot. Starting player has cue ball in hand. In certain games, however, varying combinations of the object balls are used. The rules for each different game indicate specifically which and how object balls are used.

Purpose of Game: The game can be played by individuals or sides. One individual or side seeks to pocket eight balls before the opponents. The side pocketing eight (of the fifteen) balls first wins.

Start of Play: Start of play can be determined by lagging or lot. With cue ball in hand, starting player must pocket a ball, or drive two object balls to a cushion in addition to the cue ball. In non-title play, incoming player can accept balls in position, if opponent fails to comply with rules for opening shot. In match or tournament play, starting player must pocket a ball or drive two object balls to a cushion. If he fails, opponent can accept balls in position or insist that balls be re-racked and that opening player continue to break until he complies with the rules. Player does not have to "call his shot" on opening stroke and is credited with all balls legally pocketed. In championship play only lagging is allowed to start play.

Subsequent Play: On all strokes following the opening shot, the player must call the ball or balls he intends to pocket, although he is not compelled to call the pocket.

If a ball is called, but not pocketed, other balls scored on the stroke do not count. They must be spotted. The player loses his turn at the table but is not penalized.

If a player calls more than one ball, he must pocket all balls called. If he fails, no ball is counted. If balls were pocketed, they are spotted. Player loses turn, but is not penalized.

Failure to hit a called ball is not an error, provided the cue ball touches another object ball.

If a player calls but one ball, which he pockets, he is entitled to all other balls pocketed on the same stroke.

After the opening stroke, the player must either pocket a called ball, drive an object ball to a cushion or cause the cue ball to contact a cushion after hitting object ball.

Penalties: Penalties are imposed by compelling the offending player to forfeit one ball, in addition to those pocketed on the foul stroke. If a player has no balls to his credit at the time of foul, he owes one to the table, which he must spot when he scores.

If a player fouls twice on the same stroke (such as failing to drive two object balls to the cushion on the break shot and scratching the cue ball in a pocket) only one penalty is imposed.

Player forfeits one point for:

1. Failing to comply with break shot requirements (losing one point more for each successive failure on break).

2. Scratching the cue ball in a pocket.

3. Forcing the cue ball off the table.

4. Shooting while balls are in motion.

5. Failing (after the opening stroke) to pocket a ball, causing an object ball to hit a cushion, or causing cue ball to hit cushion, after hitting object ball.

6. For striking cue ball twice on same stroke.

7. Touching cue ball or object balls with hands, cue, clothing, etc., except as on a legal stroke with cue.

Spotting Balls: Balls are spotted as outlined in general rules for spotting balls. (*See* "Rotation.")

Interference: If the balls are unlawfully interfered with in any way by the player at the table, incoming player can accept them in position or insist that original position of balls be restored.

If non-player interferes with balls, while his opponent is shooting, the offending player loses the game.

If balls are disturbed by any person or influence other than the players, conditions prior to disturbance are restored. Player at table continues his inning.

POCKET BILLIARD GAMES

General rules for pocket billiards apply unless conflicting with specific rules.

FIFTEEN BALL POCKET BILLIARDS

The Game: The game is played with a cue ball and fifteen object balls. The object balls are racked in the triangle at the foot spot. The 15 Ball is placed at the apex of the triangle at the foot spot. The next-highest numbered balls are placed near the 15 Ball, with the low-numbered balls at the back of the rack. Starting player has cue ball in hand.

Break: Start of play can be determined by lag or lot. With cue ball in hand, the starting player breaks the triangle, being required to pocket a ball or drive at least two object balls to a cushion. He does not have to call his shot.

Scoring: The purpose of the game is to score sixty-one points first. Players are credited with points corresponding to the numbers on the balls. Thus, if a player pockets the 15 Ball, he is credited with fifteen points. After the opening stroke of the game, players must pocket a ball, drive an object ball to a cushion or cause the cue ball to contact a cushion after hitting an object ball. All balls made on one legal stroke are credited to the player pocketing them. Players are not compelled to call their shots.

Penalties: On the break shot, if the starting player fails to pocket a ball or cause two object balls to go to a cushion, he loses three points, and, under option of his opponent, can be required to break the balls again. If he fails on the second break shot to pocket a ball or cause two object balls to contact a cushion, he forfeits three more points. He loses three points for each successive failure.

A player also forfeits three points if:

A. The cue ball is pocketed.

B. A ball is not pocketed and an object ball is not driven to a cushion, or if the cue ball does not contact a cushion after hitting an object ball which fails to go to a cushion.

C. He forces his cue ball off the table.

D. He shoots out of turn and is detected before he pockets a ball. (If error is not detected and player scores, he continues shooting.)

E. He interferes with the cue ball after a stroke.

F. He strokes when any ball is in motion or spinning.

G. He fails to have one foot on the floor when stroking.

If a player is guilty of one or more fouls on the same stroke (such as failing to drive an object ball to a cushion and causing the cue ball to go into a pocket at the same time) he is penalized only for one foul and loses only three points.

Tie games can be regarded as void and played over, or by arrangement the contestants can spot the 15 Ball on the foot spot, lag for the next shot and reopen play with the cue ball in hand. The player scoring the 15 Ball wins.

ROTATION

The Game: Rotation pocket billiards is played with a cue ball and fifteen object balls numbered from 1 to 15. The object balls are racked in a triangle at the foot spot. The 1 Ball is at the apex of the triangle on the foot spot. The 2 Ball is placed at the left apex of the triangle and the 3 Ball is placed at the right apex of the triangle.

DIAGRAM
NO. 2

Break: Order of play may be determined by lagging or lot. Player making first or break shot has cue ball in hand. Opening player is compelled to make the 1 Ball the first object ball. If he fails to contact the 1 Ball on the break shot, it is an error and ends his inning. Balls pocketed (if any) on shot are spotted. Incoming player accepts balls in position. The 1 Ball is first object.

Scoring: Player or side scoring 61 points first wins game. The 1 Ball is the first object ball until it is legally pocketed. The 2 Ball then becomes the legal ball; then the 3 Ball; then the 4 Ball, etc. Rules of the game require the cue ball must strike legal object ball before touching another ball. Failure is a miss and ends the inning. Balls pocketed on an illegal contact are spotted.

If a player makes a legal contact on the object ball he is entitled to all balls pocketed on that stroke, whether or not he pocketed legal object ball. For example, if a player contacted the 1 Ball, which failed to fall into a pocket, but pocketed the 15 Ball, he is entitled to the ball or balls pocketed and continues play, the 1 Ball remaining as the object ball.

The lowest-numbered ball on the table is the object ball.

Pocketing Cue Ball: If the cue ball is pocketed it is a scratch and ends the inning. Balls pocketed on stroke are spotted.

Spotting Balls: Balls pocketed illegally are spotted on the long

DIAGRAM NO. 3

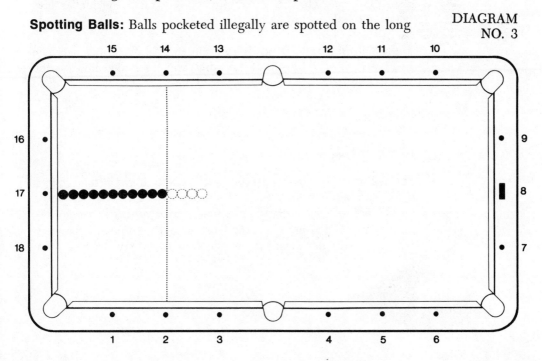

string, running from the foot spot to the center of the foot rail. Balls are spotted in numerical order. For example, if the 1 and 3 Balls are illegally pocketed, the 1 Ball is placed on the foot spot and the 3 Ball is frozen behind it on the string. If the foot spot is occupied, the spotted balls are placed on the long string as close as possible to the spot, also in numerical order. In no case is an object ball or the cue ball resting on the long string moved to make way for a ball to be spotted. Spotted balls are placed either in front or behind such object balls on the long string.

If the long string (between the foot spot and the foot rail) is totally occupied, the balls to be spotted are placed in front of the foot spot, as close as possible to the spot.

If the cue ball rests on the long string, thus interfering with the placement of an object ball, the object ball is placed either in front of or behind the cue ball, as near as possible to the cue ball without its being frozen to the cue ball.

Jumped Balls: If one or more object balls jump the table they are spotted. If player contacted legal object ball first and then caused one or more object balls to jump the table, he continues play and is credited with object balls (if any) pocketed on the stroke. If he failed to count, it is a miss and ends his inning.

If the cue ball jumps the table, it is an error and ends the inning. Balls pocketed on stroke are spotted. Incoming player proceeds with cue ball in hand.

Balls Within Head String: In rotation, if legal object lies between head string and the head of the table, and the striker has the cue ball in hand, the legal object is placed on the foot spot.

EIGHT BALL

The Game: The game is played with a cue ball and fifteen object balls, numbered from 1 to 15. Balls are racked at the foot spot, with 8 Ball in center of triangle. One player or side must pocket balls numbered from 1 to 7 or from 9 to 15. Opponent pockets group of balls not selected by player with original choice. For

DIAGRAM
NO. 4

example, if the player with the first choice chooses to score balls from 1 to 7, the opponent must pocket balls from 9 to 15. Choice of high or low group is not made until a ball is legally pocketed. Player or side pocketing numerical group first and then legally pocketing 8 Ball wins the game.

Break: Order of play can be determined by lagging or lot. Starting player is not compelled to make a choice on the opening shot, nor must he call his shot on the break. If opening player pockets a ball on the break, the group from which that ball comes shall be the object ball for that player or his side. If one ball from each group is pocketed, the opening player must then declare his group before shooting again. If the breaker fails to pocket a ball on the break, the incoming player accepts the balls in position and has his choice to shoot at any ball. No determination of object balls is made until a ball is legally pocketed.

Scoring: The striker is entitled to all balls legally pocketed, unless he pockets a ball belonging to his opponent, in which case, the opponent is credited with that ball. If player pockets only an opponent's ball and none of his own group, it is a miss.

A player must always strike one of his group of object balls first. If this is complied with, then any ball of his group pocketed on the shot is legally pocketed. If shooter strikes one of his opponent's group or the 8 Ball with the cue ball before it strikes his own object ball, the shot is not legal and any of his group made on the shot shall be respotted on the foot spot. An opponent's ball made because of this shot shall be left pocketed.

After a player has pocketed all the balls in his numerical group, he shoots to pocket the 8 Ball, calling his shot. If shooting directly at the 8 Ball (not banking), the player must pocket that ball or cause the 8 Ball or the cue ball to contact a cushion.

Loss of Game: If the player, shooting directly at the 8 Ball, fails to cause the cue ball to go to a cushion after hitting 8 Ball, or the 8 Ball to contact a cushion, he loses the game. If the 8 Ball is pocketed on the break, it is a loss of game for the breaker. If banking 8 Ball, players must hit the 8 Ball. If a player accidentally pockets the 8 Ball before he pockets all the balls of his numerical group, he loses the game.

When playing for the 8 Ball, player must hit that ball first. If he pockets the 8 Ball on a combination, where some ball other than the 8 Ball was struck first, he loses the game.

Since a player is required to call his shot when playing for the

8 Ball, he loses the game if the 8 Ball drops into a pocket not designated on the call.

When player is shooting to make the 8 Ball, he loses the game if the cue ball scratches in pocket.

Defensive Play Restrictions: When a player has some of his group of object balls on the table, any defensive shot must drive the cue ball to a rail after striking an object ball or must drive an object ball to the rail. Failure to do so will give the incoming player the option of cue ball in hand to shoot from within the head string.

Within the String: When player has cue ball in hand and object balls rest within the head string, the object ball nearest to the string is spotted on the foot spot. The same is done when the 8 Ball is the object and lies within the head string and the player has the cue ball in hand.

The following are some of the most frequently asked questions about Eight Ball rules, and the interpretation of the rules in question.

Question: If I make the 8 Ball on the break do I win or lose the game?

Answer: You lose the game because you have not complied with the basic requirement of the game, which is to pocket seven solids or seven stripes to make you eligible to shoot the 8 Ball.

Question: If I pocket the 8 Ball in another pocket than that pocket I designate do I lose the game?

Answer: You lose the game because you did not pocket the 8 Ball in the designated pocket.

Question: If I do not pocket a ball and I scratch the cue ball, do I put up a ball I have previously made?

Answer: No, you never bring a ball back to the table once it has been legally pocketed. If you have not previously pocketed a ball, you do not owe a ball because of the scratch.

Question: If I make an opponent's ball and scratch, do I have to respot the opponent's ball?

Answer: No. The penalty for the scratch is to allow your opponent's ball to stay pocketed.

14.1 CONTINUOUS
(Championship Game)

The game of 14.1 continuous pocket billiards is the game of champions—the game in which title honors in pocket billiards are decided. It is the ideal competitive game, requiring that a player have an all-around pocket billiard-playing skill.

The Game: 14.1 continuous pocket billiards is played with a cue ball and fifteen object balls, numbered from 1 to 15. Tournament play pits individual against individual, but the game could be played by partners or by teams.

Break: Contending players lag for the break. Winner of lag has option of assigning break to his opponent, which usually happens on account of the improbability of pocketing a designated ball on the break shot.

Rack: Balls are racked in a triangle at the foot of the table. It is recommended but not required that the 15 Ball be placed in the apex of the triangle on the foot spot. The 1 Ball is placed in the left apex of the triangle and the 5 Ball is placed at the right apex. The highest-numbered balls should be placed near the foot spot apex of the triangle. The lowest-numbered balls near the base of the triangle.

 DIAGRAM
NO. 5

Before a tournament or championship match opens, the referee must draw a pencil line from the foot spot to the exact center of the foot rail, thus assuring continuous accuracy in racking the balls.

Referee must also draw a pencil line on the cloth around the triangle after he places it for opening of game, thus also assuring accurate placement of the triangle for subsequent break shots. Any ball which is inside of the line or overhangs this line shall be considered to interfere with the rack.

Once a referee has racked the balls, and has stepped back from the table, he shall not rerack the balls, regardless of whether or not it is requested.

Requirements of Break: Starting player has cue ball in hand for break shot. Starting player must drive two or more object balls to a cushion in addition to cue ball or designate a ball and pocket in which that ball will drop, and then successfully accomplish this objective.

If the starting player fails to comply with the requirements of the break, the stroke is foul, he loses two points and, at the option of his opponent, may lose his inning, or, with the balls reframed, may be compelled by his opponent to break again. Opening player loses two points for each successive failure to meet requirements of break. The 15 point penalty does not apply for continued failures to legally comply with opening break rules.

If, however, opening player drives two balls to a cushion as required and scratches the cue ball into a pocket, he loses his inning, is penalized only one point and the incoming player has the cue ball in hand. This scratch does apply in the three scratch—15 point penalty.

In making the opening stroke, the breaker can shoot directly at object balls or make the cue ball touch one or more cushions before contact with the balls.

When the opening player legally breaks the object balls, without pocketing a designated ball, the incoming player accepts the balls in position.

Scoring: Game may be played to any point requirement set by officials or tournament sponsors and accepted by BCA.

In championship match play, when the defense of the title depends upon more than one block, the winning block score may be 125 or 150 or any stated number of points agreed upon by the contestants.

Assuming the block score is 125 the player who scores 125 points first wins the block, but he must continue play until he pockets all the object balls on the table but one.

If a player, after having won the block by scoring 125 points, misses in an attempt to clear the table of all object balls but one, the opponent comes to the table, clearing it of all objects but one, and the player, who cleared the table, makes the opening shot in the next block.

In subsequent blocks, the player scoring 125 points first wins the block. If, however, the winner of the second block is behind in total points for the match, play continues until one of the players has a total of 250 points, the number required for two blocks. If this situation prevails in the third block, play continues until one player has scored 375 points, and so on.

Call Shots: The game of 14.1 continuous pocket billiards is a call shot game. The player must designate the ball he expects to pocket and the pocket in which he expects to score, making his intention known to the referee, unless it is clearly obvious to the referee what the player intends. In the latter case, the referee calls the object ball. If he errs in his call, the player must correct him before striking the cue ball.

Combination and carom shots are legal in 14.1 pocket billiards.

Player need not designate other than ball and pocket in which he will make that ball. Combinations and kisses can be mentioned or designated, but have no bearing on the legality of the shot.

The player is entitled to one point for every ball called and pocketed. If he pockets the called ball and others in addition on the same stroke, he is credited with one point for each ball pocketed.

Object balls pocketed illegally are spotted on the long string. (*See* "Spotting Balls", Rotation, and Diagram 3.)

Misses: If the player misses the shot called, it is an error and ends his inning. The striker is not penalized for failing to make the cue ball contact the designated object ball, providing the cue ball hits at least one other object ball, driving this latter object ball to a cushion or into a pocket, or providing the cue ball hits a cushion after hitting an object ball. If the player, however, misses the designated object ball and fails to contact another object ball, driving the latter to a cushion or into a pocket, or if he fails to cause the cue ball to hit a cushion after it hits an object ball that isn't driven to a cushion, it is a foul, ends the inning and the player loses one point.

Continuous Play: In 14.1 continuous pocket billiards, a player may pocket fourteen balls successively. The fifteenth ball remains on the table as a break ball. The referee then racks the fourteen pocketed balls, leaving the space at the foot spot vacant in the triangle. A second cue ball may be placed as the fifteenth ball in the foot spot apex of the triangle to assure accurate framing of the balls and then removed after the rack is taken off the balls.

Player then continues making the ball outside the triangle the break ball. His procedure is to pocket the break ball in a designated pocket and carom the cue ball from the break ball into the triangle of racked balls. Player may carom cue ball from break ball into one or more cushions and then into rack. However, player is not compelled to shoot at break ball. He may, if he chooses, strike any ball in rack. (Rules for misses apply, *see* above.)

If player pockets break ball or calls and pockets shot in rack he continues play. Player can continue counting fourteen balls, having them reracked and breaking until he misses, scratches or scores the required number of points for game.

Marking Position of Balls: At the conclusion of the block in match play, the referee marks the position of the cue ball and the position of the lone object ball with a pencil, indicating the number of the next block. For example, if the players have concluded the sixth block, the referee, when marking the position of the cue ball and object ball, places a 7 where each ball rested on the table. Thus, the balls are marked for the opening shot of the seventh block.

Final Block: In the final block, play ceases when player pockets the ball that brings his total to the specified number of points to win the match.

Ball Frozen to Cushion: A player forfeits one point if when playing at an object ball frozen against a cushion, he stops the cue ball in front of such object ball, even though he contacts object ball. When playing such a shot (as a safety measure), the player must pocket the object ball, causing the cue ball to contact a cushion after striking object ball, or drive the object ball to another cushion.

If an object ball is frozen to—or within a ball width of a cushion, referee to determine by measurement, each player shall be allowed only two legal shots in safety procedure on this ball. On the third shot the player shall be forced to either drive the object ball to a different rail or drive the cue ball to any rail after contact with the object ball. Failure to do so will result in racking all fifteen balls. The cue ball shall be in hand and the player committing the infraction shall be forced to break as at the opening of the game. (*See* "Break Shot Requirement" rule.)

Note: If one of the players, resorting to the safety procedure cited above, acquires three scratches before the two-shot limit or as a result of his two shots in the safety procedure, he is penalized 1 point for each scratch and 15 points for three consecutive scratches. The three-scratches-in-succession penalty rule then applies. (*See* Loss of Fifteen Points.) It should be noted that a player is allowed only two shots in this circumstance whether the shots be legal or foul.

Cue Ball Within the String: Since, when the cue ball is in hand, the player must place the cue ball within the head string, he loses his inning and forfeits one point, if he shoots after having been warned by the referee that the cue ball is not within the string. Incoming player accepts balls in position or can insist conditions be restored to what they were before opponent fouled. If the cue ball is not within the string and the player shoots and counts before the foul is detected, he receives credit for balls pocketed and continues play. If he misses, it merely ends his inning.

Frozen Cue Ball: When the cue ball is in contact with an object ball, player may play directly at object ball in contact with cue ball, provided the object ball is moved and the cue ball strikes a cushion, or provided the object ball which is in contact with the cue ball is driven to a cushion. Failure to comply with this requirement is a foul. Penalty: loss of one point.

Foot on Floor: When shooting, the player must have one foot touching the floor. Failure is a foul. Penalty: loss of one point.

Interference: If a player accidentally disturbs in any manner the cue ball or an object ball with his necktie, coat, his hand or any part of his body or clothes, he has fouled. He loses his inning and forfeits one point.

If a player touches the cue ball or an object ball with any part of the cue other than the tip it shall be declared a deliberate foul. The offender shall be penalized 15 points and required to break as of the opening break.

When a player catches or touches a ball as it is headed for a pocket or toward the rack, he is charged with a deliberate foul and penalized 15 points. The rules for 15 point fouls applies and the game goes back to original break.

Balls in Motion: A stroke made while the cue ball and/or object balls are in motion or spinning is a foul. Penalty: loss of one point. Incoming player can accept balls in position or insist previous conditions (to foul) be restored. Referee is sole judge in restoring balls to position.

Penalties: Penalties are paid by deducting points from the offending player's score.

If a player fouls and has no points to his credit, the fouls are charged against him and deducted from his score after he counts. On the running score, his record can show —one or —two and so on. If a player wins the game while his opponent, failing to score, has two penalties against him, the score would read 150 to —two. If a player, for example, has fifteen points to his credit and then loses a point through a penalty, his score reads fourteen until he legally counts in subsequent innings.

Safety Play: Safety play is legal. The player may or may not declare his intention to play safe to the referee. If it is obvious to the referee that a player resorted to safety without declaring his intention, the referee announces "safety" after the balls stop rolling.

In attempting a safety, player must drive an object ball to a cushion, pocket an object ball, or cause the cue ball to strike a cushion after contacting object ball. Failure is a foul. Penalty: loss of 1 point.

Loss of Fifteen Points: When a player has scratched, he loses his inning, forfeits one point and a notation that he has one scratch against him is posted on the scoreboard in full view of the players and referee. The scratch is not in any way affected by opponent's play. Offending player must remove the scratch either by pocketing a ball at his next turn at the table, or by playing a legal safety. If he scratches during his next appearance at the table, without first pocketing a ball or playing a legal safety, he loses his inning, forfeits another point and "two scratches" against him are posted on the scoreboard. Again the offending player may remove the scratches by pocketing a ball, obviously trying to pocket a called ball, or playing a legal safety during his next inning. If he fails to do this and scratches for a third time in succession, he loses one point for the third scratch. plus 15 points for the three successive scratches, and is required, with cue ball in hand, to break the balls as of the opening break shot. (In other words, players lose a total of 18 points for three successive scratches.) In making break shot after three successive scratches, rules for break shot apply. (*See* Requirements for Break, Championship Game.)

Ball Bouncing from Pocket: If an object ball falls into a pocket and then rebounds on the table, it is not to be considered a pocketed ball. If the ball in question is the called ball, the player loses his inning. The ball remains in play where it comes to rest on the table.

Jumped Balls: If the cue ball jumps off the table, it is a foul. Player loses inning and forfeits one point. A scratch is marked against him. Incoming player has cue ball in hand.

If the called object ball jumps the table, it is a miss and ends the player's inning. Retrieved object ball is spotted. If the player scores the called object ball and then, as the result of the stroke, causes another object ball to jump the table, the re- trieved ball is spotted, the player is credited with the ball legally counted and continues play.

The lighting fixtures, when placed directly over the table, shall be considered part of the equipment. Should a ball leave the table, strike the lighting fixtures and then return to the table, it remains in play where it comes to rest. No penalty applies.

If a ball jumps the table, rides a rail and then returns to the table, it remains in play where it comes to rest. It is not con- sidered a jumped ball. No penalty applies.

If a ball leaves the table and comes to rest on a rail, without returning to the table bed, it is considered a jumped ball. Rules for jump balls apply, depending upon whether the ball is the cue ball or an object ball.

Jump Shots: Jump shots may or may not be illegal, depending on the following:

1. If a player causes the cue ball to jump (rise from the bed of the table) accidentally, as the result of a legal stroke, or deliberately, by elevating the butt end of the cue and striking the cue ball in the center or above center, the jump is legal.

2. If, however, a player digs under the cue ball with the tip end of the cue, causing the ball to jump, the stroke is foul. Penalty: loss of 1 point.

Object Ball Within String: If a player has the cue ball in hand and the object balls on the table are within the head string (between the head string and the head of the table) the object ball closest to the string is spotted on the foot spot. If two object balls appear to be equidistant from the string, the lowest- numbered ball is placed on the foot spot. Player, with cue ball in hand, plays from any point of his choosing within the head string, shooting at the ball on the foot spot.

Cue Ball in Hand: The cue ball is in hand at the beginning of the game, also when forced off the table or pocketed, and when for any reason fifteen balls are framed (except as superseded by the following "interference" rules): The cue ball remains in hand until the player drives it from within the head string to any point on the table between the head string and the foot of the table.

Interference with Racking of Balls: Whenever by accident or design, a player, by one stroke legally pockets the fourteenth and fifteenth balls of a frame, he is entitled to both balls, the fifteen object balls are reframed, and the player continues play from where the cue ball came to rest.

Interference with Rack: If an unpocketed ball (the fifteenth of the frame) interferes with the racking of the fourteen balls, the unpocketed ball is placed on the head spot.

If the cue ball and the unpocketed object ball interfere with the racking of the fourteen balls, the fifteen object balls are racked and the player has the cue ball in hand.

If the cue ball interferes with the racking of the fourteen object balls, the following applies:

1. The cue ball is in hand if the break object ball (outside the rack) is not within the head string (between the head string and the head of the table).

2. If break ball is within the head string, the cue ball is placed on the head spot.

3. If the break ball or fifteenth ball rests on the head spot or interferes with any ball being spotted on the head spot then the cue ball is placed on the center spot.

In any event, as a result of interference with racking the fourteen balls, the player has the option of shooting at break ball (providing it has not been racked) or any ball in the rack. If the player elects to shoot into the rack, he must drive an object ball to a cushion, or cause the cue ball to hit a cushion after contacting an object ball or pocket a ball. Failure is a foul. Penalty: loss of 1 point.

Outside Interference: Ball accidentally or deliberately disturbed by a person other than the player at the table must be replaced as near as possible to its position before interference. Player continues his inning.

Stroke Is Complete: A counting stroke cannot be regarded as complete until all the balls on the table have come to a dead stop. This rule also applies to spinning balls. Player who shoots while the cue ball or an object ball is in motion or spinning, is guilty of a foul. Penalty: loss of 1 point.

Spotting Balls: Whenever balls are being spotted on the foot spot they shall be placed as near as possible to other balls which shall mean frozen to. However, when the cue ball is interfering with the spotting of balls, the ball shall be spotted as near as possible without the ball being frozen to the cue ball.

Disqualification: If the referee considers a player to be taking an abnormal amount of time between strokes or in determining the choice of stroke with the intention of upsetting his opponent, the referee shall warn the player that he runs the risk of disqualification if he pursues these tactics. Continued disregard of the warning shall be proper grounds to disqualify the player and award the contest to his opponent.

Right to Disqualify: The right to disqualify a player in a game or from the tournament rests with the referee and/or the tournament management. Either has the power of disqualification, if there is evidence that the player was guilty of unsportsmanlike conduct during a game or of conduct during the tournament which is detrimental to the best interests of the sport. The disqualified player forfeits all right to prize money, other compensation and expenses.

Time Limit on Protests: If a player, in the opinion of his opponent, is guilty of a foul, the opponent may ask for a ruling by the referee. Complaining player, however, must enter his protest before player, allegedly making foul, shoots again after foul. Complaints registered after a subsequent stroke cannot be honored.

The following are the most frequently asked questions about 14.1 and the interpretations of the rules in question.

Question: If on the break I drive the cue ball to the foot rail—it hits the rack and stops—two object balls go to the rail—have I completed a legal break?

Answer: No. After striking an object ball or balls, the cue ball must then continue on to strike a rail. When the cue ball stops after contact with the object ball you have failed to meet the requirements of the opening break and your opponent has the option of accepting or rejecting the break. You are still assessed a two point penalty for the foul. On a subsequent break of the balls (not an opening break), such a safety play as described would be legal.

Question: If I call a ball for a certain pocket and it caroms off another ball but still goes into the designated pocket, is the shot legal?

Answer: Yes. The only requirements are that the balls go in the designated pocket. It might go around the table once or twice, hit several balls or rails. As long as the ball goes in the pocket designated, the shot is legal.

Question: If an object ball is touching the head string but is in front of the string and the cue ball is in hand, can I shoot that ball?

Answer: So long as the base of the object ball is in front of the head string you can shoot at that object ball.

LINE-UP POCKET BILLIARDS

This game is played with fifteen object balls, numbered from 1 to 15, and a cue ball. Object balls are racked on the foot spot, as in 14.1 continuous pocket billiards. Starting player has cue ball in hand. It is a call shot game, players being required to call the ball and the pocket.

Each ball legally pocketed gives the scorer credit for 1 point. All balls pocketed on a legally called shot count, the player getting 1 point for each ball.

Game is an agreed upon number of points—it can be 25, 50, 100, or whatever score agreed upon.

Start of Play: Rotation of play can be determined by lag or lot. Winner of lag has option of breaking or assigning break to his opponent.

It is possible to score nine points, as the result of all the possibilities mentioned above, on the same shot.

If a carom from an object ball stands the shake bottle on its base, player wins game automatically as the result of having accomplished this feat.

When a player has scored exactly thirty-one points, he must announce his total before an opponent takes his turn at the table. If he fails to do so, he cannot announce his victory until time for his next regular turn at the table. If, in the meantime, another player scores exactly thirty-one points and announces his victory, this latter player is the winner of the game.

Placement of Objects: At the start of the game, the 1 Ball is placed at the foot cushion at the left diamond on the foot rail. The 2 Ball is placed against the foot cushion at the right diamond on the foot rail. The shake bottle is placed open end down on the center spot. Starting player has cue ball in hand (that is, he must play it from a spot of his choice within the head string).

Start of Play: Any number of players may engage in bottle pocket billiards. Rotation of play can be determined by lagging or by drawing numbered balls from the shake bottle.

Starting player is not compelled to call his shot, but he must make either the 1 or the 2 Ball his first object.

Subsequent Play: On all subsequent shots, a ball must be the player's first object. The bottle never becomes the direct object of the cue ball until after cue ball has contacted an object ball.

If an object ball hits the bottle before the bottle is contacted by the cue ball, the shot does not count.

If the designated spot for the one or two balls is occupied after that ball has been legally pocketed, then the ball is to be spotted on the center spot. If the center spot is occupied then the head spot is used.

Upset Bottle: Whenever the bottle is upset, it must be placed upright (open end down) as close as possible to where the open end of the bottle lay when the upset bottle came to rest.

When the bottle is forced off the table or into a pocket, the player loses his turn. The bottle is spotted on center spot as of start of game.

If an object ball forces the bottle to a cushion, into a pocket or off the table, the player loses his turn.

Fouls: A foul shot (*See* general pocket billiard rules and bottle game requirements) ends the player's inning, points scored on the stroke are not allowed, and in addition, the player forfeits one point.

Starting player must pocket a called ball in the rack or drive two object balls to a cushion. Failure to do so is a foul. Offending player forfeits two points. Opponent can require that offender break again until he complies with the break shot requirements. Player loses two points for each successive failure.

Subsequent Play: After the legal break shot, if starting player has not scored, incoming player accepts balls in position. He must call his shots—ball and pocket—on all strokes. Player continues until he misses. At the conclusion of his inning, he records his points, and all balls he scored are spotted on the long string line. (*See* Diagram 3.)

If player scores all fifteen balls, they are spotted on the string line and he continues play, shooting cue ball from where it came to rest after preceding stroke.

Penalties: When a player fouls, he is penalized one point. Only one penalty is imposed, however, if the player fouls more than once on the same stroke.

General Rules: The rules for 14.1 continuous pocket billiards apply to line-up pocket billiards. Balls scored on foul strokes do not count. Penalties are paid out of the player's score. If he has no points at time of foul, he owes a point, which is deducted after he scores.

BOTTLE POCKET BILLIARDS

This game requires two object balls, numbered 1 and 2, a white cue ball and a shake bottle.

Scoring: Game consists of 31 points. Player making that total exactly wins. If, however, he scores more than 31 points, it is a miss, ends his inning and his score becomes only the points he scored over 31. If, for example, a player, exceeding 31 points, scores 35, he ends his inning, and his score becomes 4, or the difference between 31 and 35.

Scoring is accomplished as follows:
1. Carom on two object balls counts one point.
2. Pocketing the 1 Ball counts one point.
3. Pocketing the 2 Ball counts two points.
4. Carom from ball which upsets shake bottle counts five points.

Foul shots result when:
1. Player fails to hit object ball on a stroke.
2. Bottle is upset by object ball, cue, hand, clothing, etc.
3. Cue ball is forced off the table or pocketed.
4. Cue ball upsets bottle before hitting object ball.
5. Player shoots without one foot touching the floor.

General Rules: Except as they conflict with special requirements of this game, the general rules for pocket billiards apply.

COWBOY POCKET BILLIARDS

This game, a combination of carom and pocket billiards, is played with three object balls and a white cue ball. The object balls are numbered 1, 3 and 5

Start of Play: To start the game, the 3 Ball is placed on the foot spot; the 5 Ball is placed on the center spot, and the 1 Ball is placed on the head spot. Starting player has cue ball in hand and must put it in play within the head string. The 3 Ball is the first object ball.

Scoring: The winning score is 101 points.

The first 90 points are scored as follows:

1. Carom on two object balls, one point.
2. Carom on three object balls, two points.
3. Pocketing one or more object balls, points awarded according to the numerical value of the balls pocketed.

The 5 Ball, for example, gives the player five points, etc.

After a player scores exactly ninety points, the balls must come to rest on the table. Player must make the next ten points by caroms only.

After scoring 100 points, the player must score the 101st or game-winning point by caroming the cue ball off the 1 Ball into a pocket designated (call shot), without hitting a second object ball before the cue ball goes into the pocket. If the cue ball drops in a pocket not called, the player loses his turn and loses points made in that same inning.

A player also loses all points scored in an inning, if he loses his turn as the result of a foul.

Special Rules: When an object ball is pocketed it must be replaced on its original spot.

If the spots are occupied, the pocketed balls are held out (remain off the table) until the spots become unoccupied.

If the 1 Ball is pocketed, however, when a player with exactly 100 points is playing, he can have the balls spotted as of the opening of the game and play the cue ball from hand within the head string line.

Since a player with 90 points must make the next ten points by caroms, he loses his turn and points scored in that inning, if he pockets an object ball while counting from 91 to 100, inclusive.

Except as provided in the requirements of making the 101st point, the player loses his inning and point scored in that inning if he pockets the cue ball.

Player loses turn and points scored in that inning if he forces cue ball off the table.

After a cue ball scratch, incoming player has cue ball in hand. He must put it in play behind head string line and drive it to an object ball or a cushion outside the head string.

When a player has 100 points, he loses his turn and all points made in that same inning, if he fails to hit the 1 Ball in an attempt to make the 101st point.

When shooting away from a frozen object ball (when cue ball is frozen to object ball), the player must move object ball and drive the cue ball to a cushion. If he fails, it's a scratch. He loses turn and points made in that inning.

Loss of Game: If a player pockets the cue ball twice in succession without touching an object ball on either attempt, he must forfeit the game.

General Rules: Except as they conflict with the above game provisions, the general rules for pocket billiards apply.

CRIBBAGE POCKET BILLIARDS

This game is played with fifteen object balls, numbered from 1 to 15, and a white cue ball. Object balls are racked on foot spot in any order. Starting player has cue ball in hand.

It is possible score 8 points in cribbage pocket billiards although a player may win before accounting for that number, since his opponent may have points to his credit. For example, if an opponent has 3 points, and a player scores 5, the latter wins the game.

Each point is called a "cribbage".

Start of Play: Rotation of play may be determined by lag or lot. Starting player is required to comply with break shot requirements of 14.1 continuous pocket billiards. Fouls are penalized by a 1 point forfeit in this game.

Scoring: Opening player is not required to call his shot. Any ball pocketed accrues to his credit, unless he fails to comply with the following requirements. If opening player fails to break as required by the rules, he forfeits 1 point and can be compelled to break again. If he misses, incoming player accepts balls in position.

A Cribbage: To score a cribbage (or 1 point) player must pocket two balls in the same inning, the numerical value of which totals 15. If, for example, he pocketed the 6 and 9 Balls, his total is 15 and he gets credit for a cribbage.

No more than two balls may be pocketed for a cribbage count. For example, if a player scores the 3, 7 and 5 Balls, for a count of 15, it does not count. It is an error and ends his inning. Balls are spotted.

The two balls pocketed to total a cribbage must be scored in the same inning. If a player pockets the 1 Ball, and then scratches, misses or forfeits while shooting for the 14 Ball, he ends his inning. The 1 Ball is spotted.

Since, under the scoring requirements, the 15 Ball remains on the table after all possible cribbages are scored, the player who scores the 15 Ball gets a point or a cribbage.

Balls pocketed on legal cribbages remain in the pockets.

If a player scores a cribbage legally, he can continue his inning and attempt to score one or more cribbages in the same inning.

CUTTHROAT (ELIMINATION) POCKET BILLIARDS

The Game: The game is played with a cue ball and fifteen object balls numbered from 1 to 15. It is played by three players and is quite enjoyable as a party or family game.

The Break: Start of play can be determined by lag or lot and the order of play determines the assigned balls. The breaker or first player is assigned balls 1 through 5; second shooter has balls 6 through 10; with third player having balls 11 through 15.

Balls are racked at the foot spot with the 1 at the front of the triangle, 6 and 11 on the two rear corners.

Purpose of the Game: The prime purpose of every shooter is to pocket the balls assigned to the other two players. There is no sequence requirement, and the pocketing of any object ball gives the shooter the right to continue his turn. Sometimes he may even pocket one of his own group to get better position on a ball from the other players' group.

Combinations: Combinations are not legal unless a shooter uses one of his own group as first object ball. Kiss shots are legal at all times. Should a shooter pocket one of his own group as a result of an illegal shot it stays off the table, but any opponent's ball pocketed as a result of an illegal shot is brought back to the foot spot.

Penalties: Whenever a shooter scratches or knocks the cue ball off the table he is penalized by having one of each of the other two players' groups brought back to the table at the foot spot. If there are none of the other players' groups already pocketed then the penalty does not apply. When no ball remains from a certain player's group, that player is eliminated. He must await a scratch or the conclusion of a game, before he gets another turn.

Conclusion of Play: When only one player's group or a ball or balls from one player's group are left on the table, the game is completed and that player is declared the winner. The sequence of play for the next game is determined by the order in which players have been eliminated. The first player who lost his group must rack the balls for the next game. Second player eliminated will shoot second and have the 6 through 10 and the winner of the game will break and has balls 1 through 5.

RULES FOR "ELIMINATION"
(A Variation to Include More Players)

1. This game is played by three or five players, each playing individually, on a regulation pocket billiard table.
2. Fifteen balls are racked in triangle, no special placement of any balls.

   When three players are in game:
   Player No. 1 has group of balls numbered 1 to 5
   Player No. 2 has group of balls numbered 6 to 10
   Player No. 3 has group of balls numbered 11 to 15

   When five players are in game:
   Player No. 1 has group of balls numbered 1 to 3
   Player No. 2 has group of balls numbered 4 to 6
   Player No. 3 has group of balls numbered 7 to 9
   Player No. 4 has group of balls numbered 10 to 12
   Player No. 5 has group of balls numbered 13 to 15

3. Object of game is to eliminate all balls from the table except

your own. Last player with his group or part of his group on the table is the winner.

4. Except where noted in the following rules, the general rules of Pocket Billiards as listed in the Official Rule Book apply to this game.

5. Player can shoot at any ball he wishes, including his own. Any ball accidentally pocketed stays pocketed (except if player fouls). It is not necessary to call ball or pocket. Player continues shooting until he misses.

6. If player pockets a ball or balls and fouls by scratching cue ball in pocket or off table, any balls pocketed on the shot are respotted.

7. If a player's group of balls are pocketed, he stops shooting until someone wins the game.

FORTY-ONE POCKET BILLIARDS

The Game: Forty-one pocket billiards is played with a cue ball and fifteen object balls, racked for the start of the game in the same manner that the object balls are racked for 14.1 continuous pocket billiards.

The game also requires the use of the leather shake bottle and small balls, or "peas," which are generally numbered from 1 to 15.

Rotation of play is determined by throwing each player a small ball from the bottle. The player with the lowest number must break.

Before play starts, each player is thrown another numbered ball from the bottle. This is his "private number," which he keeps secret.

Purpose of the Game: The purpose of the game is to score sufficient points (corresponding to numbers on pocketed balls) which, when added to the player's private number, total exactly 41. The player accomplishing this purpose first, declares himself the winner, proving his victory by addition.

Scoring: Players take their turn according to the first numbers thrown to them, the lowest-numbered player taking the first turn.

A player is allowed only one shot in an inning (whether or not he counts). He is entitled to all balls pocketed on one stroke in an inning.

As players score, the numbers on their pocketed balls are added to the private number.

After a player has a count of exactly forty-one he wins the game. Game is declared also when all the balls are pocketed before any player has forty-one. In this event the player closest in count to forty-one wins.

Specific Game Rules: A miss (*See* "14.1 Continuous Pocket Billiards") or pocketing the cue ball is a scratch. The offending player owes a ball to the table, besides balls he may have scored on the shot. If he has more than one ball to his credit, he can spot any ball he chooses. If a player owes a ball and has none in his rack, he must spot the first ball he legally counts. Should he pocket more than one ball on a shot (when he owes one to the table) he can spot the one of his choice.

If a player gets more than forty-one points, it is a "burst," and all the balls he has scored must be spotted. The last ball pocketed must be placed on the foot spot or as near as possible behind it.

A player who bursts can have a new private number if he chooses, resuming play in turn as at beginning of the game.

If a player resorts to safety play, he must cause the cue ball to hit a cushion either before or after contacting an object ball. Failure to do so is a scratch. Offending player owes a ball.

A player making a burst and not declaring it is disqualified from further play in that game.

General Rules: General rules for pocket billiards apply to Forty-one Pocket Billiards, except as they conflict with specific rules cited above.

GOLF POCKET BILLIARDS

The Game: Golf Pocket Billiards is played with a white cue ball and an object ball. The object ball may be any one of the fifteen object balls used in regular pocket billiards—that is, the 1 Ball, the 8 Ball, the 15 Ball, or any ball from the rack. The object of the game is to play six "holes" of golf billiards in the fewest strokes possible.

Break: On the break shot, the white ball is placed on the center spot and the object ball is placed on the foot spot. Rotation of play may be determined by lag or lot.

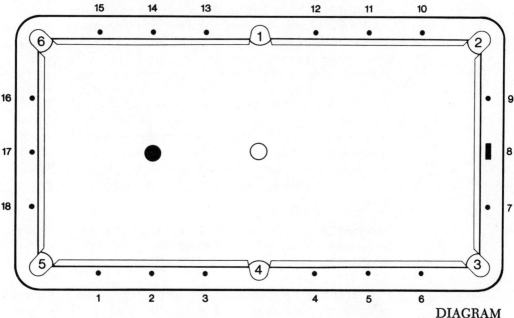

DIAGRAM
NO. 6

First Object: The starting player is compelled to bank the object ball against the foot cushion on the first stroke, attempting to pocket the ball in the left-hand side pocket. If he misses the bank shot on the first stroke, he continues to shoot until he pockets the ball, shooting either directly at the object ball or banking it, as he chooses. After the first stroke, player is not compelled to bank. When he pockets the ball, he counts the number of strokes needed to accomplish his purpose, and notes that as his score for the first "hole."

Second Player: The second player comes to the table, then, and finds the balls again spotted—the cue ball on the center spot and the object ball on the foot spot. He must bank to the lower rail on his first stroke, attempting to pocket the ball in the left-hand side pocket. If he misses on the first stroke, he can shoot either directly at the object ball or bank it until he makes the shot. His strokes amount to his score for the first "hole."

Subsequent Holes: After each player makes the opening shot, the object ball is again spotted and the cue ball is in play where it came to rest on the table after the second player scored the opening shot.

The first player then comes back to the table, and is required to pocket the object ball in the upper left-hand corner pocket, either directly or by banking (banking is not compulsory on this shot). The number of strokes required to pocket the ball is the total of the player's score for the second "hole." The second player, finding the object ball spotted again, must score it in the same pocket, playing the cue ball on the first stroke from where it came to rest after the first player completed his inning.

The object ball is spotted and the cue ball is played from where it came to rest as the players pocket the object ball in the upper right-hand corner pocket, the right-hand side pocket, the right-hand lower corner pocket and finally to the left-hand lower corner pocket. The pockets are the object-holes in that order.

Scoring: The player who completes the six holes of golf billiards in the fewest number of strokes wins the game. Each player has an equal number of innings at the table.

Partners: When playing partners, the partners' scores are added to make the total number of strokes required by the side to complete six holes of play. The side with the fewest strokes wins.

When playing partners, one partner makes the opening stroke. If he misses, the other partner comes to the table and attempts to pocket the ball. They alternate thus, until the ball is pocketed in the designated hole. If, however, one partner pockets the ball on the first stroke, that ends the side's inning. Partner who did not play in that inning makes the first stroke in the next inning.

Specific Rules: After the opening hole, the cue ball is always played from where it came to stop after the preceding stroke.

Players scratch when they pocket the white ball or pocket the object ball in the wrong pocket. Penalty is the addition of three strokes to the offending player's score, plus one stroke for the shot. Only one penalty is assessed if a player double scratches on the same stroke—that is, if he pockets the object ball in a wrong pocket and scratches the cue ball at the same time. Scratched balls are spotted and offending player continues play.

On every shot player must either pocket the object ball as designated, or cause the object ball to touch a cushion, or cause the cue ball to touch a cushion after hitting the object ball. Failure to do so is a foul and adds three strokes to the player's score, plus one stroke for the shot. Offending player continues his inning, accepting balls as he finds them.

If, when the cue ball is spotted, the object ball lies within the head string, the player may shoot directly at the object ball in that position. In other words, he does not have to spot the object ball.

General Rules: General rules of billiards apply in this game, unless conflicting with specific game rules cited above.

"MR. AND MRS." POCKET BILLIARDS
(Boy Meets Girl)

This game is played with fifteen object balls, numbered from 1 to 15, and a white cue ball. Object balls are racked at foot spot as in rotation. (*See* Diagram 2.) Starting player has cue ball in hand. The game is a combination of rotation and basic pocket billiards.

Reason for Game: This game has been devised for mixed play— that is, play by men and women. It encourages women to play pocket billiards, since the requirements of a woman player in the game make it easier for her to score than the requirements for men.

The game tends to equalize the skill of players. It can be played by men (or women) only, with the better players following rules laid down for men, and the less skilled players following the requirements laid down for women.

Start of Play: Rotation of play can be determined by lag or lot. Starting player has cue ball in hand within the head string. Balls are racked as in rotation. Starting player must make 1 Ball at foot spot apex of triangle the first object ball. He or she is credited with all balls scored on the break shot if the 1 Ball is contacted first by the cue ball.

Subsequent Play: After the break shot, men players are required to play rotation pocket billiards—that is, they must make balls the objects in numerical order. (*See* rotation pocket billiards.) Women players are not compelled to play rotation. They may make any ball the first object and are credited with all balls pocketed on a legal stroke. They do not have to "call their shots." All balls pocketed on kiss shots or combinations count for the player, but the man, playing rotation, must have hit the numerical object ball first.

Scoring: Players get points corresponding to the numbers of balls pocketed to their credit. The 5 Ball, for example, gives the player or side five points, etc.

Sixty-one points is game.

Spotting Balls: If a man pockets an object ball, not having hit first the numerical object ball, the pocketed ball or balls on that stroke are spotted. It ends his inning.

If any player scratches the cue ball in a pocket, the object balls pocketed on that stroke are spotted and the inning ends.

Balls are spotted in numerical order, from the foot spot back toward the foot cushion, as in rotation.

Cue Ball Scratch: If the cue ball is scratched in a pocket and no object balls are pocketed, the offending player loses his turn, but there is no penalty. Incoming player has cue ball in hand.

If the incoming player is a man and his numerical object ball is within the head string, the numerical object ball is spotted and man plays with cue ball in hand.

If a woman is the incoming player with cue ball in hand she may shoot at any object ball of her choice.

General Rules: Except as conflicting with above game provisions general rules for pocket billiards apply.

ONE-AND-NINE BALL

The game of One-and-Nine Ball pocket billiards is played with a cue ball and fifteen object balls, with the rules of 14.1 continuous and rotation pocket billiards applying. Balls are racked as in rotation. *See* Diagram 2.

One-and-Nine Ball pocket billiards is a four-handed game. Players determine order of play by lagging for the break.

Purpose of Game: Balls are pocketed in rotation. Player who scores the 1 Ball automatically becomes the partner of the player who scores the 9 Ball. If the same player scores the 1 and 9 Balls, he becomes the partner of the player who pockets the 10 Ball, or the 11 Ball, if the 10 Ball is off the table. The partners who score sixty-one points first win the game.

In Case of Tie: If, when all the balls are pocketed, each side has sixty points, the player who pocketed the last ball places that ball on the foot spot and has the cue ball in hand within the head string. He continues his inning. Play continues until one side pockets the lone ball on the table.

NINE BALL POCKET BILLIARDS

The Game: The game is played with a cue ball and nine balls numbered 1 through 9. Balls are racked in a diamond on the foot spot with the 1 Ball at the apex of the triangle and on the spot the 2 Ball on the left corner; 3 in the rear corner, 4 on the right corner and the 9 Ball in the center of the diamond behind the one ball. The object of the game is to legally pocket the 9 Ball—with the person or side accomplishing this purpose being declared the winner.

The Break: Option of break is determined by lag or lot. Person winning lag or choice can then determine whether he wishes to break or have his opponent break. When the opening shooter strikes the 1 Ball first the shot is legal and anything pocketed shall be scored for the shooter. From this point the shooter must always strike the lowest numbered object ball on the table. If this basic rule is complied with and no other fouls occur then anything pocketed is considered legal. No ball that has been legally pocketed shall be returned to the table as a result of fouls. Penalties shall be loss of turn only. When incoming player cannot hit lowest numbered ball on the table directly he must go to a rail and attempt to strike the ball first.

Optional Shoot Out Rule: When agreed before starting play the following rule may be in effect. If incoming player cannot hit the lowest numbered ball on the table directly, he may roll the cue ball to a spot where the ball can be hit. His opponent then has the option of shooting or making the incoming player take the shot. If the incoming player takes the shot and fails to hit the lowest numbered ball then his opponent has the cue ball in hand, and can start from any position on the table to shoot at the lowest numbered object ball on the table.

In all cases of consecutive games—loser of game becomes breaker in next game.

ONE POCKET

The Game: The game is played with a cue ball and fifteen numbered balls. The balls are racked with a regular triangle at the foot spot of the table. Option of break is determined by lag or lot, and prior to the opening shot one pocket at the foot of the table is selected by the winner of the lag as the pocket he will use, the other person or side will then use only the other pocket at the foot of the table.

The Break: The opening player may try to legally pocket any of the fifteen object balls in the pocket he has chosen. A ball pocketed elsewhere is not considered legally pocketed and is returned to the foot spot. A player continues shooting until he does not legally pocket a ball in his designated pocket. When shooter misses, the incoming player accepts the balls in position and tries to pocket any of the object balls in his designated pocket. First player to legally pocket eight balls in the pocket assigned him shall be declared the winner of the game.

In all cases of consecutive games, loser of game becomes breaker in next game. A legal safety as per rules of 14.1 must be played on each defensive shot. On the opening break only the cue ball or one object ball must be driven to the rail after initial hit.

If a player pockets a ball in his corner and at the same time pockets another ball in a pocket other than his opponent's, it is respotted after the shooter's inning has been completed. If this ball being held is the winning ball it is spotted after all balls are off the table. The shooter still in his turn at the table continues to play. If he misses, then his opponent has rightful turn to pocket the winning ball. Play continues until winning ball is legally pocketed.

A GLOSSARY OF POOL TERMS

Angle The relation of the cue ball to its target ball, known as the object ball.

Sometimes the cue ball glances off one ball to sink a second ball, known as a carom. Here the angle is between the first and second balls.

Angle also applies to the deflection of a ball from the cushion.

Angled You are angled when the corner of the pocket prevents you from shooting in a straight line at your object ball.

Around the Table A position where the cue ball must be driven to three or more cushions before hitting the object ball.

Balance Point The point at which your cue balances perfectly on your finger.

Balk The area between the head string and the head of the table. An object ball is in balk, for example, when it lies within the head string and the player has the cue ball in hand. He must shoot forward of the balk line, which means that he can hit the object ball only indirectly.

Balk Line The line on the table which defines a balk (in the above case, the head string).

Ball in Hand The cue ball is in hand at the beginning of the game, when shot into a pocket, or forced off the table, and for other reasons. The player may place it anywhere he pleases behind the balk line.

Ball Off A ball which has jumped off the table, which is a foul.

If a ball jumps the cushion, rolls along the rail and returns to the cushion, it is not a jumped ball.

If a ball leaves the cushion and comes to rest on a rail, it is a jumped ball.

Ball On A ball is said to be "on" when a player can shoot at it in a direct line.

Also, a ball is said to be "on" a pocket when it can be sunk in that pocket.

Balls Struck Simultaneously A player may strike balls simultaneously in call shot pool provided the player calls both ball and pocket.

Banded Ball The balls numbered 9 through 15 are white balls with a broad colored band equidistant from the numbers on each side.

The balls 1 through 8 are a single color, numbered but without a band.

Bank A rebound from a cushion.

Bank Shot A shot where a player banks the cue ball before sinking the object ball, or drives the object ball into a cushion and then into the pocket.

Basic Bridge The hand bridge used by all good players. The cue fits snugly into a channel formed by the thumb and the forefinger touching, which gives much greater accuracy to the stroke.

Bed The flat surface of the table.

Billiard Another word used for a carom, a shot where the cue ball glances off one ball and goes on to hit another.

Billiards A game involving nothing but caroms, played with three balls on a table without pockets.

Bottle Pool A game in which the leather shake bottle is placed on the center spot, using two object balls, numbered 1 and 2, and a cue ball. Pocketing the 1 or 2 Ball gives one or two points; a carom on the two balls gives one point; and a carom from the ball which upsets the shake bottle counts five points. Thirty-one points makes game. See Rules, page 171.

Boy Meets Girl A family game which is a combination of Rotation and Straight Pool. The man must play his balls in rotation, i.e., in the sequence of the numbers. The woman may shoot any called ball. The numbers on each pocketed ball are added up, and sixty-one points makes game. See Rules, page 171.

Break The opening shot in any game.

Break Ball In Straight Pool, or 14.1, the break ball is the last ball left on the table after fourteen balls have been sunk. The shooter tries to leave it in such a position that, after reracking the fourteen balls, he can sink this break ball and drive the cue ball into the new rack, to break up the balls.

Breaker The man who shoots the opening shot.

Breeze To hit the object ball very thinly. This is also known as feathering the ball.

Bridge The way the player's hand is placed on the cue stick to guide the tip of the cue.

Bridge, Mechanical A cue-like stick with a notched plate on the end. This is used in place of a hand bridge where the distance is too great, or where there is too much difficulty in shooting over another ball.
    Also known as The Crutch, Ladies' Aid, Old Man's Aid.

Bumper The rubber on the bottom of the cue, which saves the cue butt from wear when it is rested on the floor.

Bust Slang for break shot.

Butt The lower end of the cue.

Called Ball The ball a player announces that he will sink.

Called Pocket The pocket into which a player announces he will sink. Also known as a "Called Ball".

Carom When a cue ball glances off the object ball into a second, or even third, ball, it is a carom.
    Used as a verb, it means "glance off", i.e., carom off a ball or a cushion.
    Also known as a "kiss", or to "kiss off" a given ball.

Carrying Case   A case used to carry the cue, usually built for the cue butt and two shafts.

Center Spot   The spot in the exact center of the table, on which the cue ball or an object ball may be spotted.

Clock Dial Method   The method used in this book to designate the point at which the player strikes the cue ball, such as 1:30 o'clock, 9:00 o'clock, etc.

Combination Shot   This is the chain reaction in which the cue ball sets in motion one or more intervening balls, the last of which strikes the object ball.

Contact Point   The point at which the cue ball actually touches the object ball. Due to the curvature of the balls, it is not always the spot at which you aim. See Shot No. 1, page 27.

Count   The score, either 1 point or a number of points. In some games it is the number value of the balls pocketed.

Counting String   The string above the table, with sliding markers to keep each player's score.

Cowboy Pool   A game played with the object balls numbered 1, 3 and 5, and the cue ball. The 3 Ball is placed on the foot spot, the 5 Ball on the center spot, and the 1 Ball on the head spot. The shooter has the cue ball in hand. The object is to carom off two balls, or three balls, or pocket one or more object balls. After ninety points, the remaining points must be made by caroms only. See Rules, page 171.

Cribbage Pool   A game played with fifteen balls, as in Straight Pool. Each point is called a cribbage, and to score a cribbage (one point) a player must pocket two balls in the same inning which total 15—say, 7 and 8, or 5 and 10. The 15 Ball (also one point) must be shot last. The player with the greatest number of cribbages out of the rack wins. See Rules, page 171.

Cripple   A ball left so near a pocket it is almost impossible not to sink it.
     Also called a "minnie", a "natural".

Crown   The four dark points, or prongs, which appear on many cues above the wrapping of the handle.

Crutch   Slang for the mechanical bridge.

Cue Ball   The all-white, unnumbered ball which is the only ball struck with the cue stick.

Cue-Behind-Back   When a right-handed player has a left-handed shot, or vice versa, he sometimes turns his back to the table, and shoots with his best hand.

Cue Stick   The tapered stick with which the player strikes the cue ball.

Cue Tip   The leather button attached to the end of the shaft of the cue.

Cushion   The cloth-covered rubber buffers which line the inside rails of the table.

Cut   To hit the object ball with the cue ball at less than full center, deflecting it off at an angle.

Cutthroat Pool   A three-handed family game. The breaker is assigned balls 1 through 5, the second shooter 6 through 10, the third 11 through 15. Each shooter seeks to sink the balls of the other two players (he may sink one of his own, to get better position). When no ball remains from a player's group, he is eliminated. The last man wins. See Rules, page 171.

Dead Ball   A ball that stops dead upon contact, the result of a stop shot.

Dead Ball Shot   A shot that stops the cue ball dead when it hits the object ball.

Dead On   When two frozen balls point directly into a pocket, they are said to be "dead on".

Dead Stroke   A phrase used when a player is stroking magnificently. He is "in dead stroke."

Diamonds   One of the eighteen inlays set in the rails of a pool table, used as references or targets in making shots.

Dot   Another word for diamond.

Double Kiss   When the cue ball rebounds from the object ball into the cue tip.

Draw   A stroke in which the cue ball, struck below center, reverses its path after striking the object ball.

Draw Shot   A shot in which draw is applied to the cue ball.

Eight Ball   A game in which one player must pocket the un-banded balls from 1 to 7, and his opponent must pocket the banded balls from 9 to 15. The 8 Ball is pocketed last, and is the money ball. See Rules, page 171.

English   English is the spin of the cue ball either to the left or the right. It controls the action of the cue ball either before or after it hits the object ball or the cushion. (Some players refer to draw or follow shots as English, which is confusing.) See English, page 55.

Fancy Shot   Usually a trick shot, an exhibition shot, with pre-arranged balls. These are rarely encountered in real play.

Feather   To cut a ball very thinly. To "breeze" a ball.

Feel of a Cue   A beautifully balanced cue has a sweet "feel" to it, as opposed to a cue with too heavy a butt, too light a butt, or improper balance.

Ferrule   The one-inch segment of the cue below the tip, usually made of ivory, buckhorn, or plastic, to prevent the shaft from splitting.

Follow   Striking the cue ball above center, which produces forward spin, and causes the cue ball to roll forward in the same direction. The opposite of the draw stroke.

Follow-Through   The "follow" of the cue, after it has struck the cue ball, through the area which was occupied by the cue ball. Proper follow-through is the basis for a good stroke in pool.

Foot of Table   The end of the table not marked by the manu-facturer's name plate. The balls are racked at the foot of the table.

Foot Rail   The rail at the foot of the table, which is not marked by the manufacturer's name plate.

Foot Spot   The spot at the foot of the table, half way between the center spot and the foot rail.

Foot String   An imaginary line drawn straight through the foot spot and the two nearest diamonds on the side rails.

Forced Draw   A very powerful use of draw, putting maximum back-spin on the cue ball.

Forced Follow   A very powerful use of follow, putting the maximum forward spin on the cue ball.

Forty-One   A game played with fifteen balls, requiring the use of a leather shake bottle filled with small numbered balls, or "peas". Sequence in shooting is determined by giving each player a numbered pea. The player with the lowest number must break. Each player is then given another numbered pea, which is his own "private number". The purpose is to score sufficient points which, when added to his private number, total exactly 41.

Foul   Any infraction of the rules. The penalty depends upon the rules of the specific game.

Foul Stroke   A foul in which the foul takes place as a result of the player's stroke, such as double contact of the cue tip with the cue ball (two separate strokes).

Fourteen-One Continuous   The game of the champions. After the break of the rack, each player may sink any ball in any pocket. He must call the ball and the pocket, unless both are obvious. After fourteen balls have been sunk, they are reracked, leaving the last ball on the table. The player, in sinking this, tries to break the new fourteen-ball rack, so that he can continue his run. See Rules, page 171.

Frame   One rack of balls.

Free-Stroking   Sheer pressure often causes a player to tighten up and shoot badly. When he is shooting beautifully, it is said that he is free-stroking, or in free stroke.

Frozen Two balls which are touching each other are said to be frozen. A ball touching the cushion is also said to be frozen.

Fulcrum Point The point of balance on the cue.

Full Ball Some players, in judging the cut of a shot, shoot a "half ball", "third ball", "quarter ball", etc. When you hit the object ball in the exact center, it is a full ball shot.

Gather Shot A term in position play, where the player brings the object balls into position for easy scoring.

Golf A game using the cue ball and one object ball. The object of the game is to play six "holes" of golf pool in the fewest strokes possible. See Rules, page 171.

Grip The way the player holds the butt of his cue in making his stroke.

Gullies When a ball is sunk into a pocket, it runs through a trough (gully), and into a receptacle under the foot rail.

Head of Table The end of the table marked by the manufacturer's name plate.

Head Rail The rail which carries the manufacturer's name plate.

Head Spot The spot in the center of the string, a line (either imaginary, or actually drawn on some tables) between the two center diamonds at the head of the table.

Head String A line (imaginary, or actually drawn on some tables) between the two center diamonds at the head of the table.

High Run A large number of balls pocketed consecutively without a miss.

Hit The cue strikes the object ball, but balls hit each other, or hit the cushion. In shooting for a specific ball, if you fail to get a hit it is a foul.

Hold A player puts hold on a cue ball when he applies any action which holds it back from a course it would normally take, such as a stop shot, slight draw, or throw.

Hug the Rail Action on the cue ball which causes it to bounce along the same rail one or more times, or roll along the rail.

Hustler A term applied to pool sharks who tempt less skillful players into a game for money.

Imaginary Spot In an angle shot, the cue ball, due to its curvature, does not hit the object ball where you aim, but on the contact point. Some players often aim the cue first through the object ball, to pick out this imaginary spot. See Point of Aim.

In Hand A player has the ball in hand at the beginning of a game, meaning that he can put the cue ball anywhere he pleases behind the balk line. The cue ball is also in hand after it has been pocketed, or jumps the table.

Inning A turn at the table which ends when the player misses, fouls, scores the maximum number of balls allowed, or wins the game.

In Stroke A player is said to be in stroke when he is stroking the ball well, as opposed to jabbing, jerking, or poking. See "Free Stroking", "Dead Stroke."

Ivories Slang for the balls, which once were made of ivory.

Jam Up A phrase used when everything is doing well. "He's jam up!"

Jaw The opening of the pocket on a pool table.

Joint The screw mechanism on the cue, which connects the butt of the cue to the shaft.

Jump Shot A shot which causes the ball to rise from the bed of the table. If the player elevates the butt of the cue, and strikes the cue ball in the center or above center, the shot is legal. If, however, a player digs under a ball, causing the ball to jump, the shot is a foul. See Shot No. 41.

Jumped Ball A ball which has jumped off the table, which is a foul. See Ball Off.

Key Ball In Straight Pool (14.1), the key ball is the fourteenth ball out of the rack of fifteen balls. It is called the key ball because, when you sink it, it is the key to the final position of the cue ball and the fifteenth, or break, ball. When you sink the fifteenth ball you hope to break, or scatter, the new rack.

Key Shot   The next to the last shot in Straight Pool (14.1), i.e., the shot that sinks the key ball.

Kiss   A kiss is a carom. The cue ball kisses or caroms, i.e., deflects, from one ball to another or more balls.

Lag   To determine which player has the first shot, each player *lags,* i.e., strokes the cue ball down to the end of the table and back to the head rail. The player whose lag comes closest to the head rail may elect who shoots first.

Lagging   See Above. Lagging is also known as stringing.

Ladies' Aid   A disparaging term for the mechanical bridge, also referred to as The Crutch, The Old Man's Aid, etc.

Leave   The position of the balls after a shot, from which come the terms "good leave" or "bad leave".

Leather Shake Bottle   A sewn leather bottle, filled with small numbered balls called variously "peas", "pills", etc. It is used in games like Forty-One, to determine who shoots first, and to select the numbers of the private balls (See Forty-One), but especially in the game of Bottle Pool (See Bottle Pool). Here it is placed empty on the center spot, where overturning the bottle after a carom brings a high reward.

Lie of the Balls   Sometimes used in place of leave. See Leave.

Line Up   As in Straight Pool (14.1), each player must call which ball he sinks, and into which pocket. However, at the end of each player's inning, or after a player scores all fifteen balls, the balls are spotted on the long string line.

Live Ball   A ball that is in play under the rules of a given game.

Long   When English is used so that a ball comes off a rail at a wide angle, i.e., when *natural* or *running* English is used, as opposed to reverse English, the ball is said to roll long. See English, page 55.

Long String An imaginary line running from the center of the foot rail to the foot spot. When a ball has to be spotted, and the foot spot is occupied, the balls are spotted down this line, touching each other. The long string may be extended beyond the foot spot if all space between the spot and the end of the table is occupied.

Massé Extreme application of English on a cue ball, applied by elevating the cue. If the cue is elevated to about 45°, it is a Semi-Massé. If it is elevated to 90°, it is a Full Massé. It is used for extreme, curving shots. It may also be used for extreme follow or draw shots, when the position of the balls prevents an ordinary stroke. It is rarely used in pool; and because it may rip the cushion if used by ordinary players, it is forbidden in most pool halls.

Mechanical Bridge See Bridge, Mechanical.

Miscue A stroke in which the cue tip slips from the cue ball, due to lack of chalk, a faulty stroke, a defective tip, or an attempt to apply too much spin.

Miss Failure of a player to pocket his shot, which ends his inning. It may or may not be a foul, depending on the game which is being played.

Mr. and Mrs. A family game which is a combination of Rotation and Straight Pool. The man must play his balls in rotation. The woman, as in straight pool, may shoot any called ball. Players get points corresponding to the number on each ball they pocket. Sixty-one points is game. See Official Rules, page 171.

Narrow Angle When the cue ball is struck with reverse English, as opposed to *natural* or *running* English, it comes off the rail at a narrow angle, or short.

Nine Ball A game played with a special, diamond-shaped rack which holds balls 1 through 9. The balls must be sunk in order, from 1 through 9, with 9 as the "money ball". See Official Rules, page 000.

Nip Draw Shot When the cue ball and object ball are very close together, a normal draw stroke would bring the cue ball back into the cue, which is a foul. The Nip Draw Shot is a limited jerk stroke, which gets the cue quickly out of the way. It is also called a Pinch Draw Shot.

Nominated Ball   The ball a player calls as the one which he intends to pocket.

Object Ball   The ball the player wishes to hit with the cue ball.

Old Man's Aid   A disparaging name for the mechanical bridge.

One-and-Nine Ball   A game for four people where the rules of Straight Pool (14.1) and Rotation apply. Balls are pocketed in rotation, on a partnership basis. The partners who first score sixty-one points win the game. See Official Rules, page 171.

One-Pocket   A game where one pocket at the foot of the table is selected by the winner of the lag, and the other foot pocket goes to the second player. The winner is the player who legally pockets eight balls in his own pocket. See Official Rules, page 171.

Pack   A cluster of balls. Also synonymous with rack.

Pea   One of the small numbered balls in the leather shake bottle.

Pill   Another name for one of the small numbered balls in the leather shake bottle.

Pinch Draw Shot   Another name for a Nip Draw Shot. See Nip Draw Shot.

Picquet Shot   A name used to describe a Massé Shot which applies extreme draw to the cue ball, without the cue ball having hit an object ball first.

Pocket Billiards   A somewhat more elegant name for pool.

Point of Aim   In an angle shot, the cue ball, due to its curvature, does not hit the object ball where you aim, but on the contact point. Distinguishing the point of aim from the contact point is a matter of great importance. See Contact Point.

Pool   Pocket billiards.

Positional Play   All championship players play position. By plotting their shots ahead, and controlling the cue ball through speed, English, draw, follow, or cushion rebound, the cue ball comes to rest in position for an easy shot. *Positional play is the secret of all good pool.*

Prongs The four dark points, or crown, which appear on many cues just above the wrapping.

Push Shot Shoving or pushing the cue ball with the tip of the cue, or two contacts of the cue tip with the cue ball. The stroke is legal if the referee cannot see it, i.e., if it seems to be a flowing, uninterrupted motion. The sole judge is the referee.

Pyramid The placement of the object balls in a triangle, with the apex of the triangle on the foot spot, at the start of a game. This is called racking the balls.

Rack The wooden triangle used to pyramid the balls at the beginning of a game. The same word is used to describe the pyramid after the triangle is removed. It is also used as a verb, i.e., to rack the balls.

Rail Each table has four rails: (1) The short rail which bears the manufacturer's name plate, which is the head rail; (2) The opposite short rail, which is the foot rail; (3) The two longer side rails. Rubber cushions are fastened to each rail.

Reverse English When a spinning ball strikes a cushion at an angle, if the English (or spin) widens the angle at which the ball comes off the cushion, it is Natural English, or Running English. If it narrows the angle, it is Reverse English.
  If you are shooting to the left towards a cushion, left English is Natural English, or Running English. If you are shooting to the right towards a cushion, right English is Natural English, or Running English. The ball comes off the cushion at a wider angle.
  The reverse, which gives a smaller angle, is Reverse English. See English, page 55.

Rotation A game in which the players are required to shoot and pocket the balls in their numerical order. The lowest numbered ball on the table is the object ball. The first player to score sixty-one points wins the game. See Official Rules, page 000.

Run A series of consecutive scores on one inning. If you sink twenty-seven balls, for example, you have a run of twenty-seven.

Running English Running English is also known as Natural English, and is English applied to a ball so that it caroms off a cushion at a wider angle. See Reverse English, above, for a fuller explanation, or See English, page 55.

Safety   When a shot is too difficult to make, a player may attempt a safety, i.e., a shot which leaves the cue ball in such a position that his opponent is left with a difficult or impossible shot.

Score String   The string above the table, with sliding markers to tally the score.

Scratch   Generally, an unanticipated development in a stroke, which may or may not be a foul, depending on the game rules. Pocketing the cue ball is a scratch, for example.

Set-Up   An easy shot. See Cripple.

Shaft   The upper half of the cue. The shaft is separated from the butt of the cue by the joint.

Shark   A skillful player, often used in a disparaging sense as a man who hustles for money.

Shooting the Lights Out   A much used phrase for shooting superbly.

Shooter   The player who strikes the cue ball.

Short   A ball rolls short when it comes off the cushion with reverse English, i.e., it comes off the cushion with a narrower angle.

Short Angle of Pocket   The corner of the pocket nearest the shooter, when he is pocketing the ball from a slanting angle.

Slate   The hard material under the cushion of a pool table.

Snooker—American   Snooker is an English game played on a 6′ by 12′ table, with twenty-one balls. The balls are smaller, and the pockets are smaller. It is also played on American tables. See Official Rules, page 171.

Snookered   A man is said to be snookered when he cannot shoot the cue ball directly at his object ball, because of an intervening ball or balls. This phrase is used in American pool.

Splitting the Pocket   Shooting the object ball directly into the center of the pocket, equidistant from either side.

Spot Ball   A ball placed on the head spot, center spot, or foot spot, according to the rules.

Spotting   Putting a ball on the spot, according to the rules; also, a term used when one player allows another an edge in points.

Spots   See head spots, center spots, foot spots, spotting and spot balls. Also, thin material pasted on the playing area to denote a given spot, i.e., the exact center of the head, center and foot strings.

Squeeze Shot   Any shot where the cue ball or object ball has to pass very closely by another ball to complete a shot.

Stance   The position of the body of the shooter when he addresses the ball.

Stick   Another word for cue.

Stop Shot   A shot in which the cue ball stops dead when it strikes the object ball. See Dead Ball Shot.

Straight In   A shot where the pocket, the object ball and the cue ball are in a straight line for the pocket.

Straight On   A ball is straight on when it is hit directly in the center.

Straight Pool   A term used by players to denote the game of 14.1 Continuous, or championship pool.

String   See Center String, Counting String, Foot String, Head String, Long String, Score String.

Stroke   Stroke is the way a player uses his cue to strike the cue ball, and a player with a good stroke is apt to be a fine player. His stroke is level, soft, short, and yet his cue goes "through" the ball. Players with a bad stroke jab, poke and jerk.

Thin   A term applied to a shot that barely touches the object ball.

Throw Shot   An angle shot in which English is used to throw the ball rather than cut it. A throw shot gives more control over the ball for positional play. See Shots 13 through 17.

Tip   The leather button attached to the end of the shaft of the cue.

Top Stick   The best player.

Triangle   The triangular wooden rack used for pyramiding the balls on the foot spot.

Trick Shot   A very unusual shot, usually not found in ordinary play and used only in exhibitions.

Unbanded Ball   The balls from 1 through 8 are a single color, without a band.

V-Bridge   In the basic hand-bridge, with which the player controls the cue, the cue fits snugly into a channel formed by the thumb and forefinger (see page 11). Beginners simply rest the cue in the crotch between the thumb and forefinger, which is a V-bridge. Although it gives less control, occasionally even expert players use it for certain shots.

Wing Shot   A trick shot that pockets a ball while it is still rolling.

Wrapping   The leather, linen string, etc., wrapped around the handle of most cues to prevent slippage.